STORIES
OF OUR PAST

JOSHUA SLOCUM

The Captain who Sailed Around the World

T5-CVE-774

QUENTIN CASEY

NIMBUS
PUBLISHING LTD

*For my parents, Michael and Diane, who first
took me down to the sea and introduced me to
the world of boats and sailing.*

Nimbus Publishing Limited
3731 Mackintosh St, Halifax, NS B3K 5A5
(902) 455-4286 nimbus.ca

NB1004

Printed and bound in Canada

Author photo: Sándor Fizli
Interior and cover design: Jenn Embree

Author royalties from the sale of this book will be donated to the Alzheimer Society of Nova Scotia.

Library and Archives Canada Cataloguing in Publication

Casey, Quentin, 1980-, author
Joshua Slocum : the captain who sailed around the world / Quentin Casey.
(Stories of our past series)
    Includes bibliographical references and index.
    Issued in print and electronic formats.
ISBN 978-1-77108-142-9 (pbk.).—ISBN 978-1-77108-143-6 (pdf)

1. Slocum, Joshua, 1844-1908. 2. Voyages around the world. 3. Ship captains—Canada—Biography. 4. Brier Island (N.S.)—Biography. I. Title. II. Series: Stories of our past (Halifax, N.S.)

G440.S632C38 2014   910.4'1   C2013-908110-0
                                                                 C2013-908111-9

Canada Council   Conseil des arts
for the Arts   du Canada

Nimbus Publishing acknowledges the financial support for its publishing activities from the Government of Canada through the Canada Book Fund (CBF) and the Canada Council for the Arts, and from the Province of Nova Scotia through Film & Creative Industries Nova Scotia. We are pleased to work in partnership with Film & Creative Industries Nova Scotia to develop and promote our creative industries for the benefit of all Nova Scotians.

MIX
Paper from
responsible sources
FSC   FSC® C103113
www.fsc.org

CONTENTS

CHARMED BY THE SEA

"As for myself, the wonderful sea charmed me from the first."

–JOSHUA SLOCUM, *SAILING ALONE AROUND THE WORLD*

ON APRIL 24, 1895, Joshua Slocum hauled up the anchor on his thirty-six-foot wooden sloop and began sailing away from Boston Harbor. Under full sail, with the noon whistles sounding in the background, Slocum steered his boat past the harbour ferries and out to sea.

"A thrilling pulse beat high in me. My step was light on deck in the crisp air. I felt that there could be no turning back…" Slocum later wrote in his classic account of the voyage, *Sailing Alone Around the World*. "I had taken little advice from anyone, for I had a right to my own opinions in matters pertaining to the sea." So began a three-year voyage that took Slocum around the globe and secured his spot among the all-time great adventurers: the first person to sail around the world alone.

The solo journey was remarkable for its time. And it is all the more impressive by today's standards, considering Slocum sailed without any of our modern marvels of seafaring. Slocum's kit did not include GPS, satellite communications, a depth sounder, a radio, or even binoculars. His boat, the *Spray*, possessed no engine and lacked electricity. A lantern lit the *Spray*'s cabin, and Slocum determined his location through the

(*left*) Slocum standing at the bow of the *Spray* in 1902

A view of Westport on Brier Island, 1909, much as it would have looked during Slocum's early days

positions of the sun, moon, and stars. "It was really quite simple; the age of convenience had not yet arrived," concluded American writer Walter Teller, the captain's first true biographer. "Slocum relied on himself and on the boat he made."

Slocum's grand voyage was the culmination of a life spent at sea. It was also a trip launched out of desperation. Born in Nova Scotia's Annapolis Valley, Slocum endured a hardscrabble childhood on Brier Island before taking to sea as a teenager. Starting out as a common sailor, he rose quickly through the chain of command, eventually earning the title of Master Mariner. Though he possessed only a few years of formal education, Slocum mastered seafaring navigation and proved himself a shrewd trader. As a captain, Slocum guided ships the world over—from New York to Brazil to Japan. His adventures were many: cod fishing in Russia, shipbuilding in the Philippines, and timber trading in China. He married, raised four children at sea, and prospered financially.

By the early 1880s, Slocum was the captain and part-owner of the *Northern Light*—"the finest American sailing-vessel afloat." The poor boy from Brier Island had transformed himself into a well-to-do ship captain—the "best advertised American ship-master living." Yet by the 1890s, after being hammered by a series of setbacks—including shipwreck, the death of his first wife, and mutinies (including one uprising that forced him to shoot and kill a member of his crew)—Slocum found himself unemployed and in debt. "Misfortune dogged his heels and nearly every venture he made, whether on land or sea, turned out a dismal failure," wrote Clifton Johnson in a 1902 profile. To top it off, the great Age of Sail was ending: iron-hulled, steam-powered vessels were replacing the magnificent sailing ships that had fuelled world trade for centuries. Like many captains, Slocum found himself an aging man in a fading industry—his money gone, his prestige diminished, and his skills no longer in demand.

His professional options eroded, Slocum spent a year over-hauling a derelict sailboat he found in a field in Fairhaven, Massachusetts. In 1895, with few opportunities left, he set out to sail around the world alone, a feat no other sailor could boast of. "I am not ashamed to say that when I started my enterprise I had just $1.50 to my name," Slocum once told a newspaper re-porter. "I claim only to be one of the poorest of American sailors and having nothing else to do, made a voyage!"

The captain, by his own admission, had been "cast up" from the ocean—left high and dry after a long career as a distinguished skipper. Still, in 1895, he saw the sea as his only route back to financial health and respectability. For Slocum, life on land was fraught with stress and forces beyond his control. At sea, he found comfort and peace. The sea had shaped Slocum's career,

The *Spray* under sail in Sydney Harbour, Australia, 1897

his personality, and his values from his early days on Brier Island. "I was born in the breezes, and I had studied the sea as perhaps few men have studied it, neglecting all else," he wrote in *Sailing Alone*. Sailing out into the North Atlantic on April 24, 1895, Slocum sought success and redemption in the only way he knew how: amongst the wind and the waves.

Westport on Brier Island

CHAPTER 1

THE BOY FROM
BRIER ISLAND

THE SMALL ANNAPOLIS Valley farm sat overlooking the Bay of Fundy, not far from the water's edge. From this spot—with the right wind—waves could be heard breaking on the rocky shore below. Here, in Mount Hanley, Nova Scotia, Joshua Slocombe was born in 1844. "I was born in a cold spot, on coldest North Mountain, on a cold February 20," he wrote many years later, long after changing the spelling of his last name.

Slocum's ancestors originally hailed from Massachusetts. As British Loyalists, they fled north after the American Revolution ended British rule in America. Between 1783 and 1784, a large wave of Loyalists landed on Nova Scotian shores. Among the thousands of settlers was John Slocombe, Slocum's great-grandfather. Slocombe landed at Digby and was granted a five-hundred-acre farm in Wilmot Township, Annapolis County.

The Slocombe homestead in Mount Hanley, Nova Scotia

There he constructed a "comfortable and substantial" house in Mount Hanley with a view of the Bay of Fundy. This farm later fell into the hands of another John Slocombe, Slocum's father.

A muscular man, John Slocombe stood six feet tall and weighed two hundred pounds. Although many Slocombes had earned their living from the sea, John was mainly a landsman. That said, it was while sailing along the coast, from nearby Port George to Yarmouth, that John Slocombe, twenty-one, met eighteen-year-old Sarah Jane Southern, the daughter of a Brier Island lightkeeper. The pair married and settled at the Slocombe homestead in the Annapolis Valley. It was there that young Joshua, the fifth of eleven children, first glimpsed the sea that would shape his career and take him around the world.

"The sea was fascinating to him from the first, and he liked to watch the ships sail up and down the bay," wrote Clifton Johnson in a 1902 magazine profile. "But as a child he was a farm boy, and Nova Scotia farm life was then only one remove from pioneering." Young Slocum attended classes at a one-room schoolhouse in Mount Hanley but was also expected to help on the family farm. As an eight-year-old, he had already learned to

The One-room Schoolhouse

The small school Slocum attended in Mount Hanley still stands on a quiet road leading down to the Bay of Fundy. "From humble beginnings emerged a superb seaman, destined to become the first person to sail alone around the world," states a plaque mounted to the front of the white-shingled heritage building. "His life epitomizes courage, determination, honesty and the strength to live his dreams."

guide the old grey horse, which was blind in one eye, as it pulled a harrow over the field.

Slocum's father gripped the field plough more often than a ship's tiller, but the sea ran thick in the Slocombe blood. "On both sides my family were sailors; and if any Slocum should be found not seafaring, he will show at least an inclination to whittle models of boats and contemplate voyages," he wrote in *Sailing Alone*. "At the age of eight I had already been afloat along with other boys on the bay, with chances greatly in favour of being drowned."

For much of his life, Slocum had a distant and strained relationship with his father. During one stretch, the pair went more than two decades without seeing each other. Yet in *Sailing Alone*, Slocum offered only praise for his father. "My father was the sort of man who, if wrecked on a desolate island, would find his way home, if he had a jackknife and could find a tree," he wrote. His father's ingenuity, however, could not draw a livelihood from the family farm, which was eventually written off as "sterile and unproductive." "My poor father!" Slocum wrote in a letter in 1899. "What a load he carried and how he grubbed a living, for us all." Added the son in *Sailing Alone*: "He was a good judge of a boat, but the old clay farm…was an anchor to him."

So, in 1852, the Slocombe family (including eight-year-old Joshua) moved down the Bay of Fundy coast to Westport, a

The barn on the Slocombe homestead in Mount Hanley, Nova Scotia

Sarah Jane Slocombe

Little is known about Slocum's mother, Sarah Jane. (The captain's writing rarely mentions the most important women in his life, chiefly his mother and his first wife, Virginia.) In the 1960s, reporter David Hugo travelled to Brier Island to research Slocum. "People in Westport told me that Joshua's mother was the real influence on his early years…[and] it was generally thought locally that John helped put his wife into an early grave," Hugo reported. "Her family were retired naval people and a little more civilized than the up-country Slocums…she certainly was a good deal more genteel than her husband." The locals, Hugo concluded, characterized Sarah Jane as "a sensitive long-suffering woman married to a hard man."

fishing village on Brier Island. Free from the failed family farm, Slocum's father set up a small boot shop on the Westport waterfront. Inside, young Slocum—at the age of ten—was put to work, thus ending his few years of formal education.

The task of making fishermen's cowhide boots was an unglamorous one, particularly for young Slocum, who was more interested in playing with friends and scurrying down to see new boats arrive in port. "It may be readily surmised what kind of job it was to sit for ten hours, humped up on a bench, pegging cowhides," wrote Victor Slocum in a biography of his father. "He became an expert at pegging boots, a task which he hated."

For young Slocum, life under his father's watch—and in the "despised" boot shop—was harsh. Simply put, he found "home and shop conditions intolerable." "It is not difficult to imagine the boy's thoughts as he looked on the harbor [*sic*] from his cobbler's bench," Hugo wrote. "Fishing and trading boats coming and going all the time; nobler ships from Saint John ghosting through the Fundy fogs; these were the vessels of freedom."

Slocum began to contemplate a life at sea. He also started to whittle model ships, secretly, in the family cellar. As Victor Slocum

The Brier Island boot shop as it looks today. Now a heritage property, it was here that young Slocum toiled for his father, making leather boots.

revealed, the breaking point between father and son occurred when Slocum was twelve. One particular day, Slocum was in the cellar, putting the final touches on a new model ship. His father "burst in upon him in a fury," grabbed the model and threw it to the ground. The small vessel was destroyed, its masts and rigging left snapped and tangled on the cellar floor. And young Slocum received a good "thrashing."

Shortly after, Slocum made his first attempt at escaping to sea. It failed, however, and he earned himself another beating for his misbehaviour. Eventually, though, he broke free of his land-based shackles by finding work on a nearby fishing schooner. For a time, Slocum sailed on small fishing vessels along the Bay of Fundy coast. Then, in 1860, his mother died at age forty-six. That same year, Slocum, sixteen, went to sea for good. Joined by a friend, he travelled across the Bay of Fundy to New Brunswick. In Saint John the two boys boarded a lumber carrier bound for Dublin. "The next step toward the goal of happiness found me before the mast in a full-rigged ship bound on a foreign voyage," he later wrote.

Finally free, Slocum would not return to Nova Scotia for nearly two decades.

The launch of the *Forest* from the Churchill Shipyard in Hantsport, Nova Scotia. This painting, from 1873, depicts the world of wood and canvas in which Slocum honed his seafaring abilities and established his reputation as a skilled captain.

CAPTAIN SLOCUM

THE GRITTY WORLD of nineteenth-century seafaring was quickly revealed to Slocum, even before he departed for Dublin. At the Saint John docks, Slocum and his Brier Island chum were the first aboard their Europe-bound lumber ship. The pair stowed their gear and returned above deck. There they saw other members of the crew arriving at the dock in a wagon—"most of them roaring drunk," reported Slocum's eldest son, Victor. It was the first time Slocum—a teetotaller his entire life—saw men in such a state.

Arriving in Europe, Slocum made his way to Liverpool, England, a hub of shipping in the 1800s. "In Liverpool he received his first impression of great ships and great voyages," wrote Victor Slocum. "He became acquainted with the British seaman and admired his style." From England, Slocum shipped aboard the *Tanjore*, a British ship bound for China. Holding the rank of ordinary seaman, Slocum rounded the Cape of Good Hope at the bottom of Africa, sailed through the Indian Ocean, rounded Australia, and entered the Pacific Ocean. Aboard his next vessel, the *Soushay*, Slocum was introduced to many locations in Asia, including Indonesia and the Philippines. Brier Island was a world away.

It was while on these early voyages, during his first two years at sea, that Slocum taught himself the intricacies of seafaring navigation. Chief among his topics of self-study was celestial navigation, a complex practice that involves determining a ship's position based on its relation to the sun, moon, and certain stars. Despite his lack of formal education, Slocum mastered the Euclidean geometry, trigonometry, and algebra required in celestial navigation. "It seems safe to suggest that nobody during Slocum's lifetime excelled him at the art of navigation," wrote Geoffrey Wolff in his Slocum biography, *The Hard Way Around*. "It wasn't chance that brought Slocum's vessels home."

Slocum's ambition and effort did not go unrecognized. After two years at sea, the eighteen-year-old sailor was promoted to the rank of second mate, and eventually, first mate. Slocum always prided himself on his rise from the bottom ranks. During his time there were two main routes to securing an officer's position on a British ship. The most direct path involved paying a fee and serving a set amount of time at sea. Men who followed this route, known as "apprentices," lived in quarters at the stern of the ship—the area housing officers and the captain. Ordinary seamen like Slocum worked "before the mast" and lived below deck in the forecastle, near the bow of the ship. The only way for a "foremast hand" such as Slocum to become an officer was through raw ability and hard work. "Thus I came 'over the bows,' and not in through the cabin windows, to the command of a ship," he wrote proudly in *Sailing Alone*.

A Dangerous Profession

In 1864, while sailing aboard the bark *Agra*, Slocum experienced first-hand the unpredictable and dangerous conditions that seamen faced during the Age of Sail. Out in the middle of the Atlantic, Slocum was sent aloft, high up into the ship's rigging—a web of spars, lines, and canvas. This was a treacherous position to be in. High above the deck, a sailor had to maintain a steady grip to fight the forces of a rolling sea and strong winds. Slocum was gathering in a sail when "a gust struck him and pitched him off." Fortunately a spar broke his fall, thus saving him from serious injury or death. He was, however, left with a permanent scar above his left eye.

Although Slocum rose swiftly up the ranks, he was not content with his position as an officer; he wanted to command a vessel. This goal prompted him to adopt San Francisco as his homeport. It was there that Slocum became an American citizen—or, as he described himself, "a naturalized Yankee." In October 1869, Slocum, by then twenty-five, was named captain of the *Montana*. The seventy-five-foot coastal schooner sailed between San Francisco and nearby Half Moon Bay, hauling a cargo of potatoes, oats, and barley. "In his new capacity as ship captain, Slocum proved himself highly capable of commanding a vessel and overseeing a financial enterprise," wrote Ann Spencer in *Alone at Sea*, a biography that helped clarify and correct the details of the young captain's early commands.

Slocum quickly gained the confidence of more prominent ship owners. By April 1870 he was in command of the San Francisco-based *Constitution*, hauling a cargo of cottonseeds, lumber, and shingles south to Mexico. In early November Slocum was en route from San Francisco to Sydney, Australia. It was

a voyage that greatly altered his life: the bachelor met his future bride, twenty-year-old Virginia Albertina Walker, shortly after landing in the Australian port.

Virginia was, in fact, an American girl, born in New York to an English father and a mother with Native American ancestry. Her father, William, was a "forty-niner," a prospector during the California Gold Rush of 1849. His hunt for gold eventually took him from San Francisco to the

Virginia Slocum, age twenty-three

THE Consent of *Mr Wm Henry Walker*

19 Buckingham St, Stanmore Hill, Sydney

was given to the Marriage of *Virginia Albertina Walker*

with *Joshua Slocum*

the said *Virginia Albertina Walker* being under

the age of Twenty-one years.

Jas. Greenwood Minister or Registrar.

Marriage certificate signed by Slocum and Virginia, 1871

Australian gold fields. Considering her father's extensive wanderings, it's little surprise that Virginia enthusiastically embraced the vagabond lifestyle of a ship captain's wife. "Virginia was heard to remark that as soon as she saw Josh she knew he was just the kind of a man she wanted, not the stuffy sort she saw in conventional Sydney society," noted Victor Slocum.

A Baptist minister married Virginia and the captain on January 31, 1871. On the marriage certificate, Slocum, twenty-six, was listed as a Master Mariner. (Interestingly, his residence was listed as Massachusetts. Despite his Nova Scotian upbringing, it seems Slocum considered himself, at his core, a Massachusetts man.) In early February, Slocum and Virginia departed Australia for San Francisco aboard the *Constitution*. Despite having to live in a rugged, male-dominated world, Virginia embraced life at sea.

By May, Slocum and Virginia were aboard a new ship, the one-hundred-foot *Washington*. Their destination was Cook Inlet, a large body of water in southern Alaska. In Slocum's time this

The *Washington* in Cook Inlet, Alaska

was an extremely wild and relatively unknown area. The lure of this rugged land was simple: salmon fishing. A voyage across the Pacific followed by a fishing trip in the northern bush certainly does not classify as a traditional honeymoon. Yet the Alaska trip proved Virginia to be an adventurous spirit and a good companion for Slocum. The new bride was part of a group that hiked along the Kasilof River. Virginia, carrying a Henry rifle, used a large convocation of eagles to hone her shot.

In January 1872, while living aboard ship in San Francisco, Virginia gave birth to the couple's first child: Victor. (In all, Virginia delivered seven children, most at sea, though only four of the Slocum children survived.) In Australia, in December 1873, she gave birth to her second child, Benjamin Aymar—named in honour of the ship his father helmed at the time, the *B. Aymar*. The young family lived aboard the 128-foot vessel as

The *B. Aymar*

it criss-crossed the Pacific, hauling cargo from San Francisco to Asia and back again. The Slocums's life aboard the *B. Aymar*, however, ended in the Philippines, when the ship was sold. In the capital, Manila, Slocum was commissioned to oversee the construction of a 150-ton steamship. As payment, he would receive a schooner.

Slocum chose a jungle-fringed beach outside Manila for his shipyard. Nearby, he built his family a simple house from timber, bamboo, and rattan lashings. The surrounding slopes were covered with timber, which local workers transformed into ship planking. Conditions were "primitive," Victor recalled. "Monkeys screeched and scampered from the trees as they fell to the woodsmen's axes," he wrote, noting that loggers had to watch out for boa constrictors and crocodiles. While Slocum oversaw

Victor Slocum in China

construction, Virginia was tasked with caring for her young family "on the edge of the wilderness." Now a mother of three (a daughter, Jessie, was born in June 1875), Virginia kept a vigilant watch over her children. "My mother…made the best of jungle life," wrote Victor. "The air was heavy and damp and…up through the cracks in the split bamboo flooring could crawl centipedes, scorpions, and even a small boa."

After completing construction of the steamer, Slocum received his payment: the schooner *Pato*, which he immediately began preparing for a voyage. Slocum's time on the schooner reveals much about his character, most notably his thirst for adventure and entrepreneurial flair. His voyages on the *Pato* (Spanish for "duck") began simply enough, with a few trips between Philippine islands. Then, in Hong Kong, he decided upon another fishing trip, one that would eventually take the family far north and across the Pacific.

Slocum's destination was the Sea of Okhotsk on the eastern coast of Russia, located twenty-five hundred miles away. From Hong Kong, the *Pato*—equipped with fishing gear, dories, and a crew willing to work for a share of the catch—sailed north, past Taiwan, Korea, and Japan. Fishing from two-man dories, the crew began pulling in the ample catch. Even those left on board cast hand-lines over the rail, including Slocum and Virginia. "The sinker no sooner touched bottom than you had one," Victor wrote. "Each kept a tally of his catch."

In just two weeks the schooner was fully loaded with twenty-five thousand salted cod. His catch more robust than expected, Slocum headed to the North American West Coast, where prices were high. Landing in Portland, Oregon, Slocum was not content to dump his catch with a fish dealer and decided instead to peddle the cod himself. The captain quickly trans-

A Slocum letter from May 1890, detailing his fishing trip in the Sea of Okhotsk aboard the *Pato*

formed into a door-to-door salesman; he even carried an Okhotsk cod by the tail—a sample to prove the quality of his stock. The high value of the catch enabled Slocum to pocket "a handsome profit" and easily settle up with the crew. Everyone received a cut, including Virginia. Her hand-lining efforts netted her sixty dollars, enough to buy a Singer sewing machine. "Yes sir we had a stirring voyage and altogether a delightful time on the fishing grounds," Slocum recalled in a letter from May 1890. "Every codfish that came in over the rail was a quarter of a dollar clear."

Despite the financial success of his Okhotsk adventure, Slocum decided not to repeat it. Instead, he turned his focus to the Chinese-Philippine timber trade. First, though, he needed to secure a new vessel, one better suited to hauling lumber from the Philippines to Hong Kong boat builders. In March 1878, after wintering in Portland, Slocum moved his family back onto the *Pato* and headed toward the Hawaiian Islands, where he aimed to sell his schooner.

In Honolulu he was presented with an ideal scenario for showcasing the *Pato*'s quickness: an impromptu race. A local mail schooner had just departed from the dock when an additional sack of mail was rushed to the wharf. "Heave aboard here, I'll take it out to her," Slocum declared. Casting off the *Pato*'s lines, the captain set out to catch the mail ship. Pushed along by a well-timed gust, Slocum did just that. He blanketed the mail schooner and tossed the sack aboard. "The race at Honolulu in which the *Pato* won was very exciting, the whole town turning out to see it," Slocum recalled in his May 1890 letter. The feat earned the captain and his schooner local acclaim—and an interested buyer.

Slocum finalized the deal while Virginia and the children waited aboard a ship that would take the family to San Francisco. Eventually Slocum appeared, striding down the dock with his payment in hand. Approaching his wife, he tossed a bag of gold coins in her lap. "Virginia, there's the schooner," he declared proudly. "I sold the *Pato*…for $5,000, all in twenty dollar gold pieces," Slocum wrote in 1890. "Ugh! If I had them now!"

Back in San Francisco, the captain quickly set out to find his next vessel. His search ended when he came upon the

The *Amethyst*

109-foot bark, *Amethyst*. The *Amethyst* was Slocum's fifth ship, and for the next three years he put it to use almost exclusively in the Chinese-Philippine timber trade, often hauling lumber between Luzon (the largest island in the Philippines) and Hong Kong. The huge logs were harvested from the thick forest and floated out to the waiting *Amethyst*.

The family's sojourn in the Philippines included a sad episode that weighed particularly heavy on Virginia. At some point in 1879 she gave birth to a second daughter, but in July of that year the infant died. Virginia's grief is apparent in a letter written to her mother on July 17: "My hand shakes so now I can hardly write," she told her. "My Dear little baby died the other day…. The night she died she had one convulsion after another. I gave

The Captain's Original Biographer

American author Walter Teller was the first writer to honour Slocum with a truly detailed and substantial biography. Teller's "search" for Slocum information began in the 1950s after he read *Sailing Alone*. Intrigued, Teller wanted to learn more. Over many years he corresponded with Slocum's friends and family members, including the captain's surviving children. "I talked with his widow, then in her ninetieth year," Teller reported. "I held the hand that had held the captain's."

His work produced two biographies: *The Search for Captain Slocum* (1956) and *Joshua Slocum*, an updated version published in 1971. Concluded Teller: "[Slocum] had the strength to live in accordance with his own beliefs, even when they ran counter to prevailing thought. These are qualities that make a man worth searching for." Teller's papers and correspondence—totalling thousands of documents—are now housed at the New Bedford Whaling Museum in Massachusetts.

her a hot bath & some medicine & [she] was quite quiet. In fact I thought she was going to come around when she gave a quiet sigh & was gone."

By March 1881, the Slocums were once again in Hong Kong. On March 4, Virginia gave birth to the couple's final child, James A. Garfield—so named because he was born the day James Garfield was inaugurated as the twentieth American president. Three months later, on June 23, 1881, Slocum sold his interest in the *Amethyst* and bought a one-third share in the *Northern Light*, a ship that would significantly alter the trajectory of his career. For Slocum, the next two and a half years aboard the *Northern Light* would deliver much misery, including mutiny among his sailors and a very public rebuke of his character.

The *Northern Light*

CHAPTER 3

MUTINY

THE *Northern Light* was both elegant and grand, stretch-
ing for 220 feet and boasting three towering masts and three
decks. At age thirty-seven, Slocum was the captain of a truly
impressive ocean-going vessel. In the first chapter of *Sailing
Alone Around the World*, the captain recalled his time aboard
the *Northern Light* with great pride, referring to the ship as
his "best command." "I had a right to be proud of her, for at
that time—in the 1880s—she was the finest American sailing-
vessel afloat," he wrote.

Slocum's time aboard the *Northern Light* represents the pin-
nacle of his professional seafaring career, but it also marks the
beginning of his slow decline. His tenure as the captain and
part owner of the *Northern Light* was brief—two and a half
years. At one point Slocum was regarded as the "best advertised
American shipmaster living." Yet, by the end of his *Northern
Light* tenure, the captain's reputation was tarnished and his
prospects were dwindling.

In the spring of 1882 Slocum guided the *Northern Light*
into New York, the ship's home port, following a leisurely
forty-day journey from Liverpool, England. In his account of
the trip, Victor Slocum recalled the hustle and bustle of New
York at that time. The waters around the city, he reported,
were alive with small boats, and ferry whistles filled the air.
New York's waters were swarming with boats but, increasingly,
those vessels were crafted from iron and powered by steam.

A sketch of the *Northern Light* from *Sailing Alone Around the World*

"Steam was tightening its grip, and ships like the *Northern Light* were fast becoming outmoded," concluded Walter Teller. "Those were the final hours when masts and rigging in geometric patterns towered over the city. While Slocum was reaching a personal zenith, the sun was setting on the long age of sail."

The *Northern Light* came to rest at a pier on the East River. Shortly after, a reporter from the *New-York Tribune* visited the ship. The resulting article, entitled "An American Home Afloat," ran in the June 26, 1882, edition of the paper. "A visit to her deck suggests two sad and striking thoughts, one that American sailing ships are becoming obsolete and the other that so few American sailors can be found," the reporter noted. "She is commanded by Captain Joshua Slocum who is one of the most popular commanders sailing out of this port, both on account of his general capability and his kindness to his crew." The reporter, moving below deck, continued:

Descending to the main cabin, one wonders whether or not he is in some comfortable apartment ashore…. Mrs. Slocum sat busily engaged with her little girl at needlework. Her baby boy was fast asleep in his Chinese cradle. An older son was putting his room in order and a second son was sketching. The captain's stateroom is a commodious apartment, furnished with a…library, chairs, carpets and wardrobe…. In [another] apartment are the square piano, center table, sofa, easy chairs and carpets, while on the walls hang several oil paintings….

According to Victor, the family's "unusual" life at sea was largely influenced by Virginia's touch. Each day, between nine o'clock and noon, the Slocum children assembled for school. Their lessons ranged from spelling and reading to math. Virginia, inspired by her father—an amateur actor—also had her children memorize passages of classic verse. Saturdays were devoted to cleaning, while the Sabbath was reserved for Sunday school. And despite the family's wanderings from port to port, Santa Claus always found the Slocum children at Christmas, filling the stockings they hung on the mizzen-mast in the cabin. "He never missed, no matter what the sea or the country," Victor wrote.

Slocum's stop in New York also included a family reunion. After arriving in port, he sent

An undated photograph of Virginia wearing a fur hat

Slocum the Bookworm

A sketch of Slocum reading aboard the *Spray* during his around-the-world voyage

Slocum, throughout his life, was a voracious reader. The *Northern Light*, while under his command, housed a library consisting of five hundred books—from Dickens to Darwin. His preferred poet was Tennyson; he could recite passages from Coleridge's "The Rime of the Ancient Mariner"; and he "revelled" in the tales of Sinbad the Sailor. Among his favourite books were *David Copperfield* and *Don Quixote*. "The cabin, with its orderly and well fitted bookcases, looked very much like the study of a college professor," Victor Slocum recalled.

a letter (and money) to his father in Nova Scotia, summoning the old man to the city. "Standing now in his prime…Slocum wanted his father to see what he, the son, had accomplished," concluded Walter Teller. John Slocombe, a "fiscal failure" and now in his seventies, agreed to visit his successful son. Arriving in New York, Slocombe saw his daughter-in-law and four grandchildren for the first time. He also saw his son, now a respected ship captain, for the first time in twenty-two years and likely for the last time. Slocombe died five years later.

Despite the distance of time, the reunion was described as "a happy meeting for both." "Father came down to see me in my fine ship *Northern Light*," Slocum wrote in a letter years later. "But we didn't spend our time talking about fine large ships. Our business was a quarter of a century back…. 'Joshua,' said he, 'do you remember the night in the little boat when we rowed all night on a lee-shore and the fishing vessels came into port with close reefed sail?' Didn't I remember it!" Slocum wrote.

The elder Slocombe, who stayed in New York more than a week, was not alone on the trip. Sixteen-year-old Emma, his daughter and Slocum's half-sister, also made the journey from Nova Scotia. Emma, in a letter written to Walter Teller seventy years after the trip, still recalled fondly her seven weeks spent sightseeing and visiting museums and galleries. "I seen nothing but happiness between Josh and Virginia," she wrote. "He was a kind, thoughtful man." The good cheer of the New York visit ended, however, when the *Northern Light* was guided back to sea. The coming passages—from New York to Japan and back again—would be among the most trying of Slocum's career.

In August 1882, the *Northern Light* was loaded with a cargo of case oil, bound for Yokohama, Japan. Slocum's ship was nearly ready for sea. The only remaining task involved securing a crew for the lengthy voyage. In 1882, however, that was becoming an increasingly difficult undertaking. As the *New-York Tribune* reporter noted in his profile of life aboard the *Northern Light*, fewer American men were taking to sea during this period—a trend that can be blamed on a combination of poor wages, harsh conditions, and discipline from officers that often bordered on "sadistic." The result was a noticeable drop in the quality of sailors taking to sea in the late 1800s. Crews of the period were often comprised, as Teller put it, of "drunkards, vagrants, criminals, and degenerates." "By and large, foremast hands were being re-cruited from the dregs of society," he added. "Set against them were officers who were often brutal and tyrannical." It didn't help that many sailors were tricked, intimidated or shanghaied into duty. In New York, Slocum's crew of twenty-five seamen "tum-bled over the rail," as Victor put it, most of them likely drunk.

Slocum at age thirty-nine

The *Northern Light* was not far from port when trouble started: the rudder had broken, making the ship impossible to steer. Limp and drifting, the vessel was eventually pushed to within hailing distance of a pilot boat at New London, Connecticut. "In the meantime a full-fledged mutiny had started," Victor wrote. With the ship back at anchor, the crew "openly refused" to secure the sails. Led by a sailor named Murin, the crew argued that the voyage was now complete and demanded to go back ashore. A signal for "Mutiny on Board" was quickly hoisted to alert the Revenue Cutter Service (a precursor to the Coast Guard). Slocum, meanwhile, flatly rejected the sailors' demand to head to shore. The verdict further enflamed the situation, prompting the crew to rush toward the quarterdeck, the area of the ship traditionally reserved for officers. "It was a formidable looking crowd as they came tramping aft in close formation, armed with handspikes and whatever else they could lay hands on," Victor reported.

Slocum, not to be overrun on his own ship, intercepted the mob on the main deck. With his revolver drawn, the captain barked his order: "Stop at the peril of life." Virginia, Benjamin Slocum recalled, covered her husband's back—"with a revolver in each hand." The group halted and Murin, singled out by Slocum as the ringleader, was ordered into irons. The chief mate started to shackle the mutineer when, suddenly, Murin lunged at him with a sheath knife, stabbing the mate "furiously" in the abdomen. The mate collapsed onto the deck, while Murin was thrown down and finally secured. A Revenue Cutter eventually pulled alongside the *Northern Light* and the uprising was snuffed out. Murin, the instigator, was hauled away in double irons. His victim, the chief mate, was taken to hospital, where he died two months later.

The mutiny extinguished, Slocum's attention turned back to fixing the *Northern Light*'s steering problems and getting underway as quickly as possible—with the same crew. But even Victor questioned his father on the decision to head out with the same group of sailors. "It would have been wiser to have beached the whole crew…and to have started clean," he wrote. "After getting to sea, the New London mutiny, though to all appearances quelled, broke out like a smouldering fire in one form or another during the remainder of the voyage."

Again underway, the *Northern Light* traced a route regularly followed by clippers bound for Asia. The key, for captains such as Slocum, was to use the prevailing winds and currents to move as quickly as possible to their destination. Heading east, this involved following trade winds down to the southern Atlantic. Then, pushed along by the howling winds of the Roaring Forties, clippers passed below the Cape of Good Hope, through the southern reaches of the Indian Ocean, under Australia, and up into the Pacific Ocean.

On December 10, 1882, while sailing in the mid-Pacific, Slocum's crew spotted a "small speck" drifting on the open sea. Sailing closer, they made a troubling discovery: five people— "more dead than alive"—adrift in a twenty-one-foot open boat. The weary crew consisted of five native missionaries from the Gilbert Islands, a series of small coral islands in the central Pacific. The group had been travelling between islands when

Slocum's Quick Fists

In late 1881 the *Northern Light* sailed into Liverpool, England, following a six-month voyage from Manila. The ship was spruced up after her long voyage, and Slocum arranged for a rigger to outfit the vessel with a new bowsprit. The rigger, however, arrived at the ship later than expected. "An altercation ensued on the main deck... and the captain was cited to appear in court next morning," Victor Slocum recalled. The rigger, according to Victor, walked into court "very much bandaged and attended by both a doctor and a nurse."

The case, however, was dismissed. This is not Victor's first mention of his father's quick fists. In 1878, during a train trip from San Francisco to Nova Scotia, the captain grew angry with a man he felt was bothering a female passenger. At a stop in Pennsylvania, Slocum "knocked the intruder cold," Victor wrote.

their small boat was knocked off course by a storm. When found by the *Northern Light*'s crew, the Gilbert Islanders had been at sea forty days and were more than five hundred miles from their home island. The small boat had originally contained twelve islanders, but seven perished before their vessel was sighted.

Slocum nursed the survivors back to health with food, water, and brandy. According to Victor, his father arrived in Japan with an account of the Gilbert Islanders' ordeal written up and ready to publish. Drumming up publicity in the local papers, he raised enough money (more than $750 in the first day alone) to get the five islanders back home. "Often and often," Slocum later wrote, "in the hour of great distress and bitter sufferings, the story of the Islanders has come to my thoughts, and I have said: 'My state is not yet so bad as theirs....'" The goodwill of the Gilbert Islanders episode, however, could not snuff out the ill will that existed among a portion of the *Northern Light*'s crew. As Victor wrote: "The old mutinous spirit, hatched in New London, was still smouldering in the hatches."

Slocum with the Gilbert Islanders he rescued while aboard the *Northern Light*

The situation escalated in Japan. While anchored at Yokohama, a Russian sailor went after Slocum with a knife. The captain fought off the attack and grabbed a rifle from the ship's armoury. Gun in hand, he ordered the anchor up and the sails to be hoisted. From his perch at the wheelhouse, Slocum got his ship underway.

Shortly after, while sailing back to New York, Slocum and his crew witnessed the greatest natural disaster of the nineteenth century. Plying through Indonesian waters, the *Northern Light* passed Krakatoa, an island volcano that underwent a series of massive eruptions in 1883. The biggest explosions were heard thirty-five hundred kilometres away in Australia and propelled ash many kilometres into the air. In all, more than thirty-six thousand people were killed. The *Northern Light* sailed by Krakatoa before its final eruption in August. Still, the scene was impressive. "The sea was trembling and in bubbles," Victor recalled. Benjamin Slocum said the decks of the *Northern Light* were covered with pumice stone. "Had we been three days later in that region we would have been suffocated by its fumes," he claimed.

Slocum guided his ship past Krakatoa without serious incident. But he would not be so lucky in sailing around the Cape of Good Hope. The "Cape of Storms" is well known for violent weather, and it provided Slocum a typical welcome: heavy gales and rough seas. The *Northern Light* was weathering the assault nicely until its rudder head twisted off, crippling the vessel. The crew was able to jury-rig the rudder, but not before a series of enormous waves swept over the ship, causing a large leak. The ship's pumps struggled to remedy the situation, putting the *Northern Light* in real danger of capsizing. Slocum ordered the crew to heave the cargo of hemp overboard—a desperate attempt to keep the ship upright. Rowboats were also prepared and provisioned for the expected call to abandon ship. The *Northern Light* stabilized, however, and Slocum was able to sail his ship a short distance to Port Elizabeth. The South African port served as a "haven of refuge" for Slocum and his crew, but it was also in Port Elizabeth that Slocum's tenure as captain of the *Northern Light* truly began to unravel.

The ship remained in port for two months and underwent a massive overhaul. The stopover also brought a change to Slocum's crew. Most notably, a new officer stepped on board: Henry Slater. Appearing capable, Slater was, in fact, a British ex-convict and a "magnificent scoundrel" who forged documents to secure his position on the *Northern Light*. Before the voyage, Victor alleged,

An artist's depiction of Krakatoa erupting in 1883

Slater met some of the ship's disgruntled crew at a bar. Over glasses of gin, the group devised a plan to seize the *Northern Light* and murder the captain. In his version, Slater said Slocum hired him to serve as an enforcer-type, to keep down any hint of mutiny. As Geoffrey Wolff noted, it's impossible to determine exactly what occurred aboard the *Northern Light* en route from

Port Elizabeth to New York. What is clear is that Slater was a key figure in the affair; whether he was the instigator or the victim depends on which account of the voyage is consulted.

The episode, according to all accounts, erupted when Slater bungled an attempt to adjust some of the ship's rigging. Questioned by Slocum on the matter, Slater—according to Victor—told the captain to "mind his own damned business." Faced with insubordination, Slocum stripped Slater of his rank and ordered him below deck. According to William Dimmock, a *Northern Light* officer, Slater disobeyed the captain's orders and tried to incite a mutiny. He also snatched "revolvers and cases of ammunition." (Slater admitted to grabbing a revolver, but said he later threw it overboard.) With Slater armed, Slocum deemed him "too dangerous" to remain free and had the sailor put in irons. Slater remained shackled and confined until the *Northern Light* landed in New York on November 22, 1883—a span of fifty-three days.

Slater claimed he was restrained with more than eighty pounds of chain and held in a narrow space he described as a "Black Hole." "In this 'box' I suffered the tortures of the damned, my hunger and thirst were intolerable," Slater later stated. "I begged Captain Slocum to give me water and food; but in vain." Officer Dimmock, however, categorically disputed Slater's allegations of mistreatment. "I can truthfully say that Slater never was injured

Slocum's Leadership Style

Slocum's time aboard the *Northern Light* raises questions about his style of discipline. "I'm not a martinet, but I have my own ideas of how to run a ship," he told a Boston newspaper reporter in August 1894. "I guess I have been at it long enough to know my business. The old shipmasters treated their crews like intelligent beings, giving them plenty of leeway but holding them with a strong hand in an emergency. That's my style, and that's the way to hold the confidence and respect of the men."

or brutally treated on the *Northern Light*. He was punished for his actions, and that justly deserved," Dimmock stated. "Capt. Slocum is as fine a man as ever I want to have anything to do with…he is kind, cheerful and generous to his men," he continued. "I have read the evidence against the captain in the New York papers…. They were one-sided reports, and I was disgusted with the reading of them." Slocum's apparent loss in the court of public opinion was followed by his defeat in the court system itself. Accused with "cruelly and inhumanly treating his prisoner," Slocum was convicted, fined five hundred dollars, and labelled a "brute" in the editorial pages of *The New York Times*.

That was in late 1883. But in January 1884, a bizarre twist developed in the Slocum-Slater saga. Slater gave an interview to B. S. Osborn, editor of the influential *Nautical Gazette*, in which he came "clean" about the whole affair. Slater refuted his testimony against Slocum and claimed he was unknowingly drawn into a plot to blackmail the captain. "I do not blame Capt. Slocum for the treatment I received," Slater told Osborn. In the same article, Osborn described Slocum as "an A1 man, a genuine Yankee captain of high reputation." But the damage was done. The newspaper also noted that Slocum was battling lawsuits that had emerged in the wake of the Slater episode. Tied up on shore with legal matters, Slocum was forced to find another captain to sail the *Northern Light* on its next voyage. "Capt. Slocum is a part owner of the vessel, and this has not only cost him a great deal of money…but it is calculated to hurt his reputation," the article continued. "He is brave, though, and will not let these misfortunes triumph over his future."

That optimistic prediction was later proven correct. But at the time, Slocum was struggling. Following the Slater affair, the controlling partners bought out his interest in the *Northern Light*. Slocum's "best command" had ended; his time aboard the "magnificent" *Northern Light* was over.

CHAPTER 4

A SEA OF TROUBLES

LIFE AT SEA in the 1880s was fraught with danger. As Slocum's time on the *Northern Light* revealed, the hazards were many: from rough weather to mutinous, violent sailors. For Virginia Slocum, those dangers lurked in the presence of her four young children.

Aboard her husband's ships, Virginia was an island in a sea of rough-and-tumble masculinity. And though her responsibilities centred primarily on the domestic side, Virginia's influence extended beyond the family's living quarters. In a letter from 1897, the captain remembered his wife's skill in taking "sights" with a sextant, an instrument used in celestial navigation. She could also crunch complex navigation calculations "as correctly as any one could," he noted. "Mother was a remarkable woman, not many had the stamina she had," wrote daughter Jessie Slocum in a letter to biographer Walter Teller.

In Virginia, Slocum found a partner who mirrored his adventurous spirit. Benjamin Slocum recalled his mother's passion for the outdoors. In Australia, he said, Virginia was trained to ride horses. On riding excursions she explored the countryside and "slept on the ground much as the natives did." Benjamin also recalled his mother's success in shark hunting. "It was my job to get the shark interested in coming close up under the ship's stern, where mother dispatched it with her Smith & Wesson revolver," Benjamin wrote in a letter to Teller. "She never needed but one shot."

(*left*) Virginia in the 1870s

Women at Sea in the Age of Sail

As Joan Druett revealed in her book, *Hen Frigates: Wives of Merchant Captains Under Sail*, many captains' wives took to sea during this period. Those women, like Virginia, gave birth, raised children, survived storms, and visited exotic ports—all while navigating within a male-dominated world. "Voyaging under these circumstances seems a most remarkable challenge," Druett wrote. "Yet these were ordinary, conservative, middle-class women, certainly not rebels or adventurers…seafaring was an extraordinary proposition for a nineteenth-century lady."

Virginia clearly possessed a unique blend of strength and courage. But even she was left troubled by the events that unfolded on the *Northern Light*. "Voyaging with cutthroats was to her like voyaging with a volcano under the hatches," Victor Slocum wrote. "And the nervous strain caused by the constant alarms at sea had undermined her health, for she was predisposed to a weak heart."

Following their exit from the *Northern Light*, the Slocums lived in Boston with the captain's sisters. Virginia welcomed the respite from the "mutinous turmoil" of the previous eighteen months. Slocum, meanwhile, sought out his next venture. According to Victor, his father investigated, but later rejected, the prospect of jumping aboard a steamship. Was this stubbornness or was Slocum simply a purest? Perhaps, after decades aboard wind-powered, wooden ships, he felt unequipped to shift to a world of new technology. Regardless of his thinking, the captain decided to dodge the world of steam and iron. Instead, he continued to navigate within the realm of canvas and wood—despite the sector's obvious decline.

Slocum's hunt for a new vessel led him to the *Aquidneck*, a 138-foot bark about a fifth the size of the *Northern Light*.

The *Aquidneck* under full sail

In March 1884, Slocum was listed as the ship's sole owner and master. When the wind blew, he recalled, the *Aquidneck* "asked no favours of steamers." Garfield Slocum recalled the *Aquidneck*'s "beautiful" saloon, its skylight made from coloured glass, and its grand piano. Victor echoed those descriptions, noting the *Aquidneck* was as close to a yacht as a merchant ship could be.

Departing the US with a cargo of flour, Slocum guided his new ship to Brazil. It was a "pleasant" trip, Victor reported, highlighted by a picnic in a coconut grove when the family arrived on shore in Pernambuco. That excursion, however, was likely the last such outing the Slocums enjoyed as a complete family.

From Brazil, the *Aquidneck* sailed south to Buenos Aires, the capital and chief port of Argentina. En route, Virginia became sick and retreated to bed. Garfield recalled that his mother was forced to stop her regular activities, including embroidering. "I remember the piece she worked on last," he later wrote. "She left her needle where she stopped." By the morning of July 25, 1884, Virginia was out of bed, salting butter with Benjamin. Slocum, meanwhile, was on shore trying to secure his next cargo. Virginia had recently asked her husband to take the family to her native Australia. According to Benjamin, his mother wanted the children to have a "proper education" and a home "on shore." Slocum agreed. And so, on this July day, he was seeking a cargo that would take them all to Australia.

At some point that morning Virginia's health deteriorated. Alerted to the situation, Slocum hurried back to the ship to be by his wife's side. "Father returned about noon and I was called by father at about 8 P.M. to kneel at her bedside as she breathed her last—her eyes closed and motionless," Benjamin recalled years later. It's unclear what ailment claimed Virginia so quickly. But Benjamin offered a theory. "I believe she had a weak heart. She often fainted when trouble disturbed her," he wrote. "I never cared to ask father." Regardless, Virginia was gone at age thirty-four. Slocum was now without his trusted partner and alone in raising four young children.

"Mother died [and] father was like a ship with a broken rudder," Garfield told Walter Teller. "She helped him so much." Benjamin echoed those thoughts in one of his letters. "She knew father better than all others," he wrote. "Father learned to understand her powers of intuition and he relied on it fully until she passed on. His ill fortunes gathered rapidly from the time of her death." Virginia was buried in a cemetery in Buenos Aires. A few days later, Slocum ran the *Aquidneck* aground on a sandbar. The vessel was removed, but at a hefty cost.

In February 1885, Slocum wrote a painfully sad letter to his mother-in-law in Australia, addressing her as "Dear Mother."

Virginia's grave in Buenos Aires, 1884

"My heart goes out again for your poor aching heart," he wrote. "I feel most of the time that Virginia is with me and helping me and that her noble soul is helping support her poor dear mother.... I doubt not at all that she is with you and me more now than before," he continued.

It has pained me tho [*sic*] to have to give up my beatiful [*sic*] wife…. The children are just lovely and healthy. I shall strive to do well by my loved one's children. I shall try mother to make her Happy in Heaven. She was, I know, happy with me here. She knew that I loved her dearly, and always loved to be in her company. What a terrible separation this has been to me.

Slocum also addressed his deteriorating financial situation: "I would have had some money in [hand] by this time if I hadn't got crazy and run my vessel onshore," he wrote. "As it is now I am just swimming out of trouble on borrowed money…the vessel is mine and I may be lucky enough to earn something with her…." Then he concluded: "I send you a photo of our dear one's grave. The name Virginia is in gold and shall be kept in gold as long as I live," he wrote, signing the letter, "Yours in affliction."

The plan to sail to Australia evaporated after Virginia's death. Instead, Slocum took his young family north to Boston to live with two of his sisters. "I never returned to the sea," Benjamin wrote, "father wept when I begged to be left ashore…. The ocean is no place to raise a family." Jessie and Garfield joined Benjamin. Victor, meanwhile, stayed aboard the *Aquidneck* with his father. "A decision I have never since regretted," Victor wrote years later, "for I would rather be a sailor than anything else."

Slocum, at this point, was struggling to draw a living from the sea while clearly trying to recover from Virginia's death. Benjamin said his father's sorrow was apparent during one particular visit to see the children in Boston: "He was sad and very much alone seeking company and a remedy for his lonely life." Benjamin also remembered his father looking at a photograph of Virginia: "Tears streamed over his face." Added Garfield: "When mother died…father lost interest in life."

Though heartbroken, Slocum eventually remarried. His new bride was Henrietta Miller Elliott. Hettie, as she was commonly known, was the captain's first cousin. The twenty-four-year-old had recently arrived in Massachusetts from Nova Scotia. According to one relative, the young dressmaker and seamstress was "no doubt bedazzled" by the attention shown to her by the accomplished captain, then forty-two—and nearly twenty years her senior. The pair married in Boston on February 22, 1886, a year and a half after Virginia's passing. Six days later, young Hettie set sail with her husband aboard the *Aquidneck*. Her initial journey, however, would be far from a romantic honeymoon. In fact, the voyage would be marred by setbacks and mark Slocum's last as a merchant captain.

Slocum and Hettie were joined on the ship by fifteen-year-old Victor and five-year-old Garfield. Benjamin and Jessie, meanwhile, stayed onshore with Slocum's sisters; the family was again divided. The *Aquidneck* pulled away from frostbitten New York and immediately entered a hurricane. The strong winds limited the ship's canvas to a "mere rag"—a foresail only slightly larger

Slocum, Hettie, Garfield, and Victor seated on the *Liberdade* in 1889

than a tablecloth. The crew, meanwhile, had to be lashed to their posts to ensure they were not washed overboard. "Mountains of seas swept clean over the bark," Slocum wrote. The "wild storm" quickly exposed some faulty caulking in the *Aquidneck*'s decking. With the sea boiling, water began pouring in. Slocum ran the ship's pumps for thirty-six straight hours, yet the water continued to rise. At one point the hold of the *Aquidneck* was half filled with water. With the vessel losing stability, Slocum prepared to abandon ship. Garfield recalled being placed—with Hettie—into a lifeboat stocked with provisions. "The hurricane…tried hard to send us to Davy Jones' Locker," Garfield wrote years later. "Father and the crew had to work very long hours without sleep to keep the ship afloat." The leak was eventually discovered and promptly plugged. The flow of seawater cut off, Slocum's pumps finally gained the edge.

Slocum's ship soon emerged from the hurricane winds. Ten days from New York, the *Aquidneck* was rolling along comfortably; porpoises and dolphins were playing alongside the ship as the crew dried their clothing in the trade winds. "Our hardships were now all forgotten," Slocum wrote, "for 'the sea washes off all the woes of men.'" At Rosario, an inland port in Argentina, Slocum loaded his vessel with a cargo of baled hay. This seemingly innocuous freight would result in years of grief and a significant financial loss for the captain.

Slocum's problems stemmed, in part, from the wave of cholera that was fast spreading through Argentina—"filling towns and cities with sickness and death," he wrote. The Argentinean hay was bound for Rio de Janeiro, but Brazilian officials there—fearing the spread of cholera—ordered Slocum to first take his ship to a quarantine station at Ilha Grande, a small Brazilian island. Slocum landed at Ilha Grande on January 7, 1887. The next morning, however, port officials pulled alongside the *Aquidneck* and ordered him away. The port was closed. "Leave at once," an official told Slocum. "Or the guard-ship will fire into you." So Slocum was forced to sail back to Rosario—"at a ruinous loss… of time and money."

The Brazilian ports eventually reopened, meaning Slocum could make a second attempt at delivering the hay. First, though, he had to secure a new crew. There was just one problem: the pool of potential sailors—already heavy with undesirables—was further contaminated by the release of prisoners from Argentinean jails during the cholera outbreak. "Of six who shipped with me, four had been released from prison, where they had been serving time for murder or highway robbery," Slocum wrote. "All this I learned when it was too late." It was, he recalled, the "hardest looking" crew to ever set foot on one of his ships. Despite their ill appearance, the crew helped sail the *Aquidneck* to Rio. There, on May 11, 1887, the ship was unloaded of its cargo of hay, nearly five months after originally setting out.

By July 23, the *Aquidneck* was anchored at another Brazilian port: Antonina. Shortly before midnight, Hettie woke her husband after hearing suspicious whispers and footsteps above their cabin. Armed with a repeating rifle, Slocum stepped on deck through a back entrance. Rubbing his eyes in the darkness, the captain heard a voice. "Why don't ye come on deck like a man," it said. The situation was clear: Slocum was facing another mutiny. According to Victor, some amongst the "cutthroat crew" believed there was a sizable amount of money on board. So a plan was launched to seize the *Aquidneck*.

On deck, the gang's ringleader lunged at Slocum and received the butt end of the captain's rifle. But the blow did little to slow the sailor. He soon had Slocum by the throat and was attempting to pitch the captain overboard. "I could not speak, or even breathe, but my carbine spoke for me, and the ruffian fell

Slocum and Hettie aboard the *Spray* in 1902

with the knife in his hand which had been raised against me!" Slocum recalled in his account of the voyage. With the ringleader wounded, Slocum now faced the rest of the gang, which he said approached "like hungry wolves." Another knife-wielding member of the crew sprang at the captain, but was killed instantly by a second shot from Slocum's rifle. The mutiny was over. "How it was that I regained my advantage, after once losing it, I hardly know," he wrote. "A man will defend himself and his family to the last, for life is sweet, after all." Slocum was arrested, charged with murder and detained in Antonina. He pleaded self-defense and a month later, on August 23, was acquitted and released.

The mutineers were gone, but life aboard the *Aquidneck* was not destined to improve. Back at sea, Slocum realized smallpox was quickly spreading among his crew. With few bodies available to help work the ship, he and Victor sailed the *Aquidneck* through a "mad tempest" in search of help. The gale had grown to a hurricane by the time Slocum spotted an island to anchor at. "Then wet, and lame and weary, we fell down in our drenched clothes, to rest as we might—to sleep, or to listen to groans of our dying shipmates," Slocum recalled, calling it the "most dismal" of all his nights at sea.

Receiving little assistance, Slocum had but one option: dispose of the bodies overboard. "I listened to the solemn splash that told of one life ended, and its work done," the captain recalled of his "melancholy" duty. Arriving in Uruguay, Slocum's "dejected" crew finally received a respite. The remaining sick men were taken on shore in Montevideo and the *Aquidneck* was disinfected. The operation cost Slocum more than one thousand dollars. "What it cost me in health and mental anxiety cannot be estimated by such value," he wrote.

With the recent string of hard voyages and "sad business" behind them, the family set out on a new venture: hauling Brazilian timber.

The *Aquidneck* was loaded shortly after Christmas of 1887 and set out from Paranaguá Bay with its heavy wooden freight. Almost immediately, though, the *Aquidneck* was pushed onto a sandbar by strong currents and wind. The vessel was stranded broadside to the open sea and pounded by the ocean swell. "The waves [were] dashing over her groaning hull…till at last her back was broke— and why not add 'heart' as well!" Slocum wrote. "This was no time to weep, for the lives of all the crew were saved; neither was it a time to laugh, for our loss was great." The Slocums were officially shipwrecked. "Father lost all his money and our beautiful home," Garfield recalled of the *Aquidneck*'s grounding.

It is hard to fathom that a captain of Slocum's ability and experience could lose his vessel under what appear to be relatively mild conditions. Was he truly betrayed by the local winds and current? Or was the captain at a breaking point—fatigued by recent mutinies, illness, death, jail, and, of course, the passing of Virginia? As Slocum himself noted, "many and severe disappointments" had taken a toll on his "health and nerve." Regardless of cause, the stranding of the uninsured *Aquidneck* inflicted further damage on the captain's finances. Lengthy stays in quarantine, expensive fumigations and doctors' visits had "swept my dollars into hands other than mine," Slocum admitted in his writing. "My wealth was gone."

When the *Aquidneck* ran aground, so did Slocum's career as the captain of tall-masted, ocean-going sailing ships. Though his seagoing adventures certainly continued, his remaining voyages were all undertaken aboard much smaller and far less grand vessels. Among them was the *Liberdade*, the thirty-five-foot boat the captain and his family constructed to "escape" from Brazil and return home to the US.

The small boat, which Slocum regularly referred to as a "canoe," was completely of the captain's design—a blend of features from some of his favourite ships, including Cape Ann dories and Japanese and Chinese sampans. The *Liberdade* was constructed from wood hauled from the *Aquidneck*'s cargo, as well as timber cut from the surrounding forest. The craft was put together with tools saved from the *Aquidneck*—"a meagre kit," Slocum admitted. And each member of the family contributed in some way: Victor served as carpenter and rope maker, while Hettie made the sails—"and very good sails they were, too!" boasted the captain of his wife's handiwork. Even little Garfield wielded a hammer during the construction phase. The family's new home was launched on May 13, 1888, the day slavery was abolished in Brazil. To honour the occasion, Slocum named his vessel *Liberdade*, Portuguese for "liberty."

The *Liberdade*, with Slocum standing at the stern, followed by Hettie, Garfield, and Victor, 1889

Provisioning the *Liberdade*

Before departing Brazil, Slocum loaded his new vessel with all the food and supplies necessary for the long voyage home. Here is the captain's detailed list of provisions:

Sea-biscuits, 120 lbs.; flour, 25 lbs.; sugar, 30 lbs.; coffee, 9 lbs.... Of tea we had 3 lbs.; pork, 20 lbs.; dried beef, 100 lbs.; dried codfish, 20 lbs.; 2 bottles of honey, 200 oranges, 6 bunches of bananas, 120 gallons of water; also a small basket of yams, and a dozen sticks of sugar-cane, by way of vegetables. Our medicine chest contained Brazil nuts, pepper, and cinnamon; no other medicines or condiments were required on the voyage, except table salt, which we also had. One musket and a carbine...together with ammunition and three cutlasses, were stowed away...to be used in case of necessity.

On June 24, the Slocums sailed out of Brazil's Paranaguá Bay and into the open Atlantic. The *Liberdade* skirted leisurely up the coast of Brazil to Barbados, stopping at various ports and outposts. Writing about their passage over the equator, the captain paid a veiled tribute to Virginia: "We left those [constellations] of the south at last, with the Southern Cross—most beautiful in all the heavens—to watch over a friend."

By Christmas Day the Slocums were on Chesapeake Bay, enjoying a dinner of "turkey and a bountiful plum duff." The "canoe" had carried the family from Brazil to the US—a voyage of 5,500 miles. "This was the voyage made in the boat which cost less than a hundred dollars," Slocum wrote proudly. Two days later, the *Liberdade* sailed into Washington, DC, where it was moored for the winter. "We were all very glad to haul up for the winter after our long and tiresome voyage," Hettie wrote to a friend. "It surprises me more and more when I think of all we have come through."

How did Slocum sum up the voyage? "With all its vicissitudes I still love a life on the broad, free ocean, never regretting the choice of my profession," he wrote. Slocum still adored his chosen vocation, but in the winter of 1889 it did not love him back. Though his days were still spent aboard ship, he was no longer drawing a living from his efforts.

CHAPTER 5

POVERTY POINT

FROM WASHINGTON, Slocum sailed the *Liberdade* to New York City. There, on May 18, 1889, a newspaper reporter stepped on board to interview Hettie. The resulting front-page story noted that Slocum's voyage from Brazil to America was known "far and wide." But what did Hettie—or the "Captain's captain"— think of the trip? "Are you going on another voyage, Mrs. Slocum?" the reporter asked. "Oh, I hope not. I haven't been home in over three years, and this was my wedding journey," she replied, clad in a dark blue yachting dress and a straw hat. "It is an experience which I should not care to repeat." Hettie told the reporter she planned to soon visit family in Boston. "I shall travel by rail," she said. "I have had enough sailing to last me for a long time."

If Slocum returned to sea, it would clearly be without Hettie. That is, if he could get back to sea at all. The captain gained a level of fame from his *Liberdade* adventures, but his mild celebrity status failed to help in his hunt for work. "As for a ship to command—there were not enough ships to go round," he wrote in *Sailing Alone*. "Nearly all our tall vessels had been cut down for coal-barges, and were being ignominiously towed by the nose from port to port." Concluded Walter Teller: "Within a span of five years Slocum had lost his wife, his home, his money and now, at age 45, his profession as well."

(*left*) Slocum circa 1890, around the time he self-published *Voyage of the Liberdade*

A copy of *Voyage of the Liberdade*, which Slocum self-published in Boston in 1890

Seeking Restitution

In addition to writing, Slocum sought compensation for his treatment by Brazilian officials at Ilha Grande, the quarantine station he was expelled from in 1887. Slocum pressed his case with the American government, even writing letters to President Grover Cleveland. "I have sustained a ruinous loss through no fault of mine which bids to throw me out of my home afloat," Slocum wrote in an 1887 letter to the president.

According to Slocum, his expulsion from Ilha Grande led to a spiralling chain of misfortune, including mutiny, smallpox, and his arrest and acquittal for killing a member of the *Aquidneck*'s crew. The "chapter of disasters" culminated with the *Aquidneck*'s grounding and destruction. "We have sailed on a sea of troubles!" he declared. The captain sought ten thousand dollars in damages. Despite pressing his case for six years, Slocum was denied compensation.

With Slocum struggling to find work, the family scattered in many directions. For a time, Garfield and Jessie lived with Hettie's sister in East Boston. "Father did not come to that home," Garfield wrote. "Don't know where he was, I assume that he was trying to find a job." According to Garfield, the famous White Star Line offered his father a captain's post aboard a steamer, but he turned it down. Why? "I followed the sea in sailing ships since I was 14 years old," the captain told his son. "If I accepted this offer I would have to get used to steamships, and I do not like steamships."

Landlocked and unemployed, Slocum turned his attention to other tasks, including putting his adventures aboard the *Liberdade* into story form. The result was the *Voyage of the Liberdade*, which he self-published in Boston in 1890. The thin volume revealed his skill in weaving a good sea yarn. His writing ability was impressive by any measure, but particularly so considering he was a sea

A sketch of Slocum rebuilding the *Spray* in Fairhaven, Massachusetts. The project puzzled local residents. "Great was the amazement," Slocum recalled. "'Will it pay?' was the question which for a year or more I answered by declaring that I would make it pay."

captain with little formal education. As Slocum himself noted, his hand had "grasped the sextant more often than the…pen."

The unemployed captain eventually found a job as a carpenter in an East Boston shipyard. One day, while working on a boat, a mix of coal and dirt landed on Slocum's face. "I stood up, thought of the difference between my state and when I was master of the *Northern Light*, and quit the job," he later told a newspaper reporter. The aging captain, in his own words, had been "cast up" from the ocean. "And so when times for freighters got bad, as at last they did, and I tried to quit the sea, what was there for an old sailor to do?" he wrote in *Sailing Alone*.

Slocum's prospects changed forever, however, when he decided to pour his energy into rebuilding a derelict oyster sloop. In *Sailing Alone*, he recalled a chance meeting in Boston with Eben Pierce, an old friend and retired whaling captain. "Come to Fairhaven and I'll give you a ship," Slocum recalled Pierce saying. "But," Pierce added, "she wants some repairs." As Slocum found out, that was a mild assessment of the vessel's condition.

Fairhaven, located in southeastern Massachusetts, sits across the Acushnet River from New Bedford, a former hub in the global whaling industry. Slocum recalled discovering his new vessel "propped up in a field, some distance from salt water." Fittingly, Slocum found the *Spray* in an area of Fairhaven called Poverty Point. The boat was covered with canvas and in a state of disrepair. Pierce, Slocum concluded, had played "something of a joke on me." "The 'ship' proved to be a very antiquated sloop called the *Spray*, which the neighbors declared had been built in the year 1," he wrote.

Correcting the Captain's Timeline

In *Sailing Alone*, Slocum said he arrived in Fairhaven in the winter of 1892. However, a review of newspaper clippings from the period reveals the captain was off in his recollection; he was likely introduced to the *Spray* in 1891. On November 28, 1891, the *New Bedford Evening Standard* ran a front-page feature profiling Slocum's rebuilding efforts. According to the article, Slocum—a "celebrated sailor and adventurer"—moved to Fairhaven to work at a shipyard. Slocum discovered the "dilapidated" *Spray* (described as "nearly 75 years old") near Eben Pierce's house, where he was living at the time. On May 14, 1892, the *Fairhaven Star* reported that Slocum's sloop was "nearly completed."

The *Spray* under sail in Australian waters, 1897

Regardless of when—and under what circumstances—he found his trusted ship, Slocum set out to make the "little boat…a match for any craft, in any sea." Working alone, Slocum chopped down a "stout" oak tree to serve as the *Spray*'s keel. He steamed and bent timber for the ship's ribs and hammered down thick planks of white pine for the vessel's deck. Inside, he fashioned a cooking galley, shelves for storage, space for "many months" of provisions, and a snug berth to sleep in. A mast was fashioned from a New Hampshire spruce. "Something tangible appeared every day to show for my labor, and the neighbors made the

The *Destroyer* at Pernambuco Harbour, 1893

work sociable," Slocum wrote. "The *Spray* changed her being so gradually that it was hard to say at what point the old died or the new took birth."

The overhaul complete, Slocum slapped two coats of copper paint on the *Spray*'s bottom (and two coats of white paint on her topsides) and slid his restored ship into the water. "As she rode at her ancient, rust-eaten anchor, she sat on the water like a swan," he wrote proudly. The *Spray*'s maiden voyage took place in July of 1892: a cruise across Buzzards Bay, off Cape Cod. "Sails were bent, and away she flew," Slocum wrote. In all, the captain spent $553.62—and thirteen months—rebuilding the thirty-six-foot boat that would take him around the world.

It's unclear exactly when Slocum sprung his plan for an around-the-world voyage, but the idea was formed sometime between the *Spray*'s launch in 1892 and his eventual departure in 1895. During this period Slocum scraped by—sailing aboard the *Spray* and dipping his line as an unsuccessful fisherman. "Times were hard on shore!" he wrote.

The chronology of the period is hazy, but it did include one noteworthy adventure. In 1893, Slocum was named the navigator of the *Destroyer*, a 130-foot iron warship. Slocum's task was to guide the *Destroyer* from New York to Brazil, where the Brazilian government hoped it would help quell a recent revolt. The *Destroyer*, designed to fire torpedoes, was purchased in the US and was to be towed by tugboat to Brazil—with Slocum serving as "navigator in command." The captain, it was reported in late 1893, "was highly recommended" for the position.

The winter journey, which started on December 7, 1893, in New York, was a wet one. The thirteen-man crew spent much of its time "pumping and bailing" the leaky and unseaworthy craft, which no company would insure for the voyage. "Everything is wet," Slocum wrote. "There is not a dry place in the entire ship! We are most literally sailing under the sea." In February 1884, the *Destroyer* was towed into Bahia on the Atlantic coast of Brazil, ending what Slocum called "the hardest voyage that I ever made." His "hardships and perils," however, were all for nothing when a Brazilian crew grounded the vessel on a rock shortly after its arrival. Whether the ship was scuttled on purpose or through incompetence is not entirely clear. Regardless, Slocum's chance of getting paid sank along with the *Destroyer*. Once again, he departed Brazil with empty pockets.

Slocum returned to Fairhaven by steamer and attempted to profit by committing the adventure to paper. The result was his second book, *Voyage of the "Destroyer" from New York to Brazil*, which he wrote seated in the "quiet cabin of my home on the *Spray*." Self-published in 1894, the book sold only a few copies. But it proved popular with the Boston papers. "The story reads like a romance," stated one reviewer. "It is a tale of danger, hardships and excitement from beginning to end."

Despite the encouraging reviews, Slocum could not derive a living from his writing. Instead, he turned his attention to fishing. In *Sailing Alone*, the captain said he spent a season aboard the *Spray* fishing the coast—"only to find that I had not the cunning properly to bait a hook." Out of professional options, Slocum drew up a new plan. "But at last the time arrived to weigh anchor and get to sea in earnest," he wrote. "I had resolved on a voyage around the world."

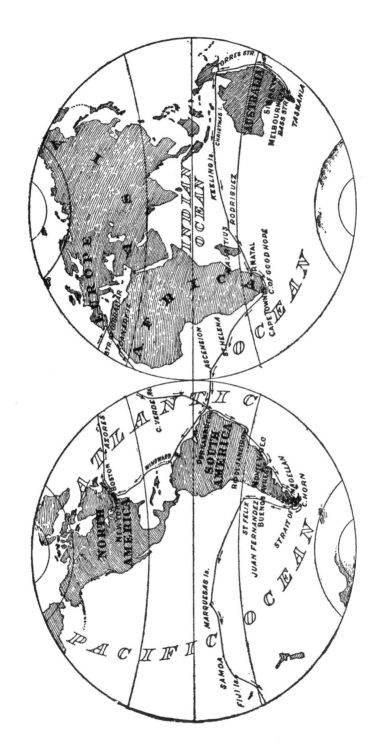

Chart of the *Spray*'s course around the world: April 24, 1895, to July 3, 1898

CHAPTER 6

AROUND THE WORLD

IN MID-APRIL 1895, Slocum was living aboard the *Spray* at a dock in East Boston, preparing his vessel for the ambitious voyage. The local papers, keen to report the details of the coming trip, sent reporters to interview the adventurer. "Capt. Josh is a kinky salt, 51 years old, as spry as a kitten and as nimble as a monkey," a reporter wrote in the April 16 edition of the *Boston Herald*. "He has circled the globe five times, and knows every sea of it. All the education he ever got was on the water, but he is an encyclopedia now." Even during Slocum's day—when people were still shuttled between continents exclusively by ship—his proposed voyage was considered dangerous, capable of making "many a hardy mariner" shrink. Slocum, however, showed "confidence" and "determination."

"The object of the trip? Well, it is mainly to make money," Slocum told a reporter from the *Boston Daily Globe*. "I see money ahead if I get through safely." He also planned to earn cash by filing regular reports to a syndicate of newspapers. He claimed deals were in place with the *New York Sun*, *Louisville Courier-Journal*, and the *Boston Daily Globe*. As for his route, Slocum planned to first sail to Central America, where he hoped to have the *Spray* hauled across the Isthmus of Panama to the Pacific Ocean (the Panama Canal was not completed until 1914). Once in the Pacific, he would head to the Suez Canal and sail through the Mediterranean Sea before crossing

Hettie: Living in Virginia's Shadow

Slocum and Hettie gardening in West Tisbury, Massachusetts, 1902

Slocum told the *Daily Globe* he planned to sail alone, "unless…my wife changes her mind about staying ashore." Hettie, likely still recalling her trying experiences aboard the *Aquidneck* and the *Liberdade*, opted—unsurprisingly—to stay on land.

Slocum's relationship with Hettie contrasted greatly with the connection he shared with Virginia. "Father's days were done with the passing of mother—they were pals," Benjamin Slocum told Walter Teller. "His later marriage did not click." Added Garfield: "Father and Hettie never talked about their troubles when I was near them…whenever I came near both of them were quiet. It was not pleasant." Regardless of his feelings for Hettie, it appears Slocum saw his round-the-world voyage, in part, as a way to fashion a proper life with her. Concluded a report in the *Boston Herald*: "He reckons it his last voyage and hopes to make enough out of it to return home to his wife and four children and buy a little farm where he may settle down."

the Atlantic for home. This proposed route, of course, was not the one Slocum followed. And in fact, he planned a variety of courses and stopping points that, in the end, did not materialize. Slocum was also off in his timeline. Predicting a two-year voyage, he stayed at sea for over three years.

Well-stocked and confident, Slocum began his grand journey at noon on April 24, 1895. "The day was perfect, the sunlight clear and strong," he wrote of the *Spray*'s departure from Boston Harbor.

"Her good angel had embarked on the voyage; I so read it in the sea." From the start, however, Slocum's progress was slow. His first stop was the fishing port of Gloucester, a short sail north of Boston. There he lingered for a full two weeks, stopping to "look the *Spray* over and again to weigh the voyage, and my feelings, and all that." Continuing north to Nova Scotia, Slocum arrived at his childhood home of Westport, on Brier Island—"The Island of Plenty." "To find myself among old schoolmates now was charming," he wrote. "The very stones on [Brier] Island I was glad to see again, and I knew them all. The little shop round the corner, which for thirty-five years I had not seen, was the same, except that it looked a deal smaller. It wore the same shingles—I was sure of it."

On May 13, 1895, Slocum wrote a letter to his editors at Roberts Brothers, the Boston publishing house that issued *Voyage of the Liberdade* and which was now serving as his agent. Despite his slow pace, Slocum insisted the voyage would prove "interesting." "Do please be patient with me," he added. By June 20, more than a month later, Slocum had only progressed as far as Yarmouth—a mere day's sail from Brier Island. Writing again to his editors, he blamed his "slow movement" on the need to make repairs to his vessel. "All the money I have been able to raise so far I have put into the *Spray*," he wrote. Before departing Yarmouth, Slocum loaded the sloop with butter, a barrel of potatoes, and six barrels of water. He also paid one dollar for a small, damaged tin clock—"the only timepiece I carried on the whole voyage."

On the morning of July 2, Slocum headed out across the "boisterous Atlantic." A month later he "discovered" Spain. After sailing into Gibraltar, the captain sat in his cabin and penned a letter to a friend in Westport. "The *Spray* came across the little old pond…as quickly as possible. Had there been even ten men onboard sailing her she could not have come more quickly,"

Slocum on the *Spray* during his stop at Gibraltar

he wrote. Yet the transatlantic voyage was not without some hardship. Sailing into the "unbounded sea," Slocum was struck by "the acute pain of solitude." "In the dismal fog I felt myself drifting into loneliness, an insect on a straw in the midst of the elements," he wrote in *Sailing Alone*. To fight his profound "sense of solitude" Slocum called out commands to an imaginary crew; it didn't help. "My voice sounded hollow on the empty air, and I dropped the practice."

The loneliness eventually passed and Slocum arrived at the Azores, a collection of volcanic islands located west of Portugal. There the *Spray* was loaded with fruit and cheese; the pairing proved a terrible combination. Back at sea, Slocum was overcome with food poisoning. Lying in "agony" on the cabin floor, he looked up to see a tall man at the helm. Donning a large red cap and sporting "shaggy black whiskers," the man introduced himself as the pilot of the *Pinta*, one of Christopher Columbus's ships.

(Slocum was at the time reading a Columbus biography.) "Lie quiet, senor captain," the pilot told a delirious Slocum. "I will guide your ship to-night." When Slocum awoke the next day, he found the *Spray* holding course and "going like a racehorse."

In Gibraltar, the British Admiral invited the captain to dock the *Spray* amongst Her Majesty's battleships. "The old craft is now the guest of Admiral ships and among guns of great calibre," he wrote proudly in his letter from Gibraltar. Slocum was offered assistance in making repairs and replacing the *Spray's* torn jib. He was also invited to dine with the local governor and provided with a steady supply of fresh milk and vegetables.

"The *Spray* came across the little old pond...as quickly as possible," wrote Slocum in this letter, which he penned after arriving in Gibraltar in 1895.

From Gibraltar, Slocum intended to sail across the Mediterranean Sea, through the Suez Canal and into the Indian Ocean. But his plans changed upon hearing reports of Red Sea pirates. Instead, he opted to re-cross the Atlantic and head for South America. On August 25, 1895, the *Spray* re-entered the Atlantic with a "toss and bound." Slocum's attempt to evade pirates, however, proved unsuccessful. Still within sight of land, he spotted a rogue sailing craft following quickly in his wake. "They were coming on like the wind," he recalled in *Sailing Alone*. "I saw by their movements that they were now preparing to strike a blow." That strike was averted, however, when a sudden squall blew through the area, dismasting the pirates' boat.

Pushed along by the trade winds, Slocum was provided time for "rest and recuperation." He spent his time reading, writing and fiddling with the *Spray*'s rigging. There was also time to cook, including meals comprised of the flying fish that accidently landed on deck. Slocum was now enjoying his "solitude supreme." Even in his dreams he was alone.

A month later, on October 5, Slocum landed

Chart of the *Spray*'s Atlantic voyages from Boston to Gibraltar, then to the Strait of Magellan, in 1895, and finally homeward bound from the Cape of Good Hope in 1898

in Brazil. His forty-day journey back across the Atlantic, he later boasted, was made with expert precision. All the Atlantic islands—from the Canaries to Cape Verde—appeared exactly where he expected they would. "I never did better when I had even the best of chronometers and officers to assist," he wrote during the voyage. Slocum's accurate positioning was all the more impressive considering he was without a proper chronometer. A chronometer is essentially a very accurate clock, used in marine navigation to help determine a ship's longitude. Slocum's only timepiece was the tin clock he purchased in Yarmouth. He referred to it as a chronometer only as a joke, noting it was "often run down or refusing duty." It also, for at least part of the journey, lacked a minute hand—thus rendering it useless as a chronometer.

Slocum's navigation was impeccable, but not all aspects of the journey were proceeding perfectly. His plan to fund the voyage by writing newspaper travel pieces was crumbling. After seven months at sea he had not yet left the Atlantic. Even by nineteenth-century standards his progress was slow. Not surprisingly, the papers in his syndicate were growing bored. Papers were either buying his copy at a lower-than-expected price, or not buying at all. By early November, Slocum was in Rio de Janeiro and his writing prospects were completely eroded. Undeterred, he wrote an upbeat letter to Eugene Hardy, the general manager of Roberts Brothers, the publishing house that was serving as his agent. "I am in the very best of health and living in great hope," he wrote.

Sailing south from Rio, the captain nearly drowned while working to pull the *Spray* off a beach in Uruguay, where he accidently grounded her. (Despite his years at sea, Slocum could not swim.) Yet the captain's biggest test of ability and perseverance was still to come. His chosen route would take him around South America and into the Pacific, requiring him to navigate some of the most treacherous waters in the world—the "wonderland of the South," as he called it.

On February 11, 1896, Slocum sailed into the Strait of Magellan, a passage between the mainland tip of South America and the island of Tierra del Fuego. Linking the Atlantic and Pacific oceans, the Strait marked an important shipping route in the days before the Panama Canal. It was also well known for its poor conditions and "tortuous" course among many islands and channels. Slocum entered the Strait to a rude welcome: a gale was throwing up foamy seas, and dangerous tidal rips surged near the entrance. Close by, a steamship lay smashed on a beach.

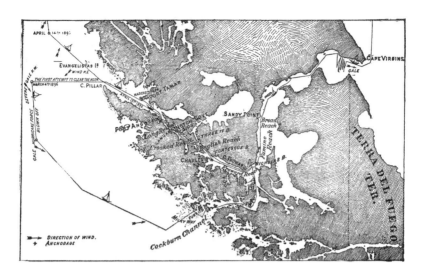

The course of the *Spray* through the wild Strait of Magellan

Pushing through the gale-force winds with tightly reefed sails, Slocum reached Punta Arenas in southern Chile, then a coaling station of two thousand hearty souls. There he was warned against continuing on in the Strait alone. The port captain suggested he ship a crew to help fight off likely attacks from natives in the area. Slocum ignored the recommendation, choosing instead to load his guns.

His vessel stocked with smoked venison and biscuits, Slocum continued on. Not far from Punta Arenas he experienced his first blast from a williwaw—a sudden, violent squall that blows offshore along mountainous coasts. By February 20, his birthday, the captain found himself alone—"with hardly so much as a bird in sight"—at Cape Froward, the southernmost point on the South American mainland. He spent his fifty-second birthday sailing against heavy squalls and a stiff current. At day's end he anchored the *Spray* and brewed himself a cup of coffee—a meek celebration, but one that helped revive his strength.

A few days later, Slocum spotted natives heading toward his boat by canoe. He was well prepared for their approach, setting up a scarecrow and changing his outfit to give the impression that a full crew was aboard. Still they paddled closer. The leader of the group, Slocum reported, was "Black Pedro"—a wanted man known as the "worst murderer in Tierra del Fuego." It took two warning shots from Slocum's gun before the group abandoned its advance. "In the Strait of Magellan the greatest vigilance was necessary," he wrote.

Battling gales, williwaws, and strong currents, Slocum pressed on. Eventually he could see the end of the Strait. Beyond it was the wide Pacific. "Here I felt the throb of the great ocean that lay before me. I knew now that I had put a world behind me, and that I was opening out another world ahead," he wrote. But it was not to be. Slocum exited the "bleak and lifeless" land only to be tossed back into it. No sooner had he "plunged" into the Pacific than he was hit by a ferocious storm. "I saw now only the gleaming crests of the waves. They showed white teeth while the sloop balanced over them," he wrote. "No ship in the world could have stood up against so violent a gale." How bad were the conditions? Rough enough to make even Slocum seasick.

Unable to hold his ground, Slocum was forced to retreat. He allowed the "great gale" to push the *Spray*—now stripped of all her sails—southward down the coast of South America. She roared past the entrance to the Strait of Magellan and in the direction of Cape Horn, the most southern point of South America. Days passed and still the *Spray* was pushed on in the wrong direction. Finally the gale subsided enough for Slocum to guide his sloop toward the shore, in the direction of the Cockburn Channel, a passage that leads back to the Strait of Magellan. From there he would be forced to retrace half of his journey through the Strait. Navigating a "mountainous sea" and narrowly avoiding foaming breakers, Slocum pushed toward the channel. This was, he said, the "Milky Way of the sea"—an area Charles Darwin once said would give any landlubber nightmares. "Hail and sleet in the fierce squalls cut my flesh till the blood trickled over my face; but what of that?" Slocum wrote proudly. "This was the greatest sea adventure of my life. God knows how my vessel escaped."

Re-entering the Strait of Magellan, Slocum was again forced to contend with strong winds and brisk currents, all while dodging sinister rocks, whirlpools, and marauding natives. Sudden williwaws again hammered the *Spray*—some so strong they dragged the sloop's two anchors. One storm even covered the *Spray*'s deck with snow as Slocum sailed passed islands and bays first seen many weeks before. "Sea-cuts in my hands from pulling on hard, wet ropes were sometimes painful and often bled freely," he wrote of his trials in the Strait. Still, he retained a sense of humour. Discovering an island not on his chart, Slocum named it after a friend and promptly put up a sign that read: *Keep off the grass.*

Finally, on the morning of April 14, Slocum sailed into the Pacific and away from the Strait of Magellan. That evening a wave broke over the captain as he stood at the helm. "It seemed to wash away old regrets," he wrote. "All my troubles were now astern; summer was ahead; all the world was again before me." Finally free from the "lonesome strait," Slocum was bound for the tropics.

Of all the items Slocum carried aboard the *Spray*, it was his books he treasured most. The *Spray*'s ample library contained volumes ranging from Shakespeare to Darwin's *The Descent of Man* to "the poems of Moore, Longfellow, Burns and Tennyson." While sailing across the Pacific, Slocum purposely steered the *Spray* to places of literary significance. The first stop on that tour occurred at the Juan Fernández Islands, a group of three nearly uninhabited islands located about 350 miles west of Chile.

Chef Slocum

Slocum on the *Spray* in an unidentified port during his around-the-world voyage

While sailing alone, Slocum served as captain, navigator, and crew. He was also the ship cook, a role he revelled in. "Of course I had to live simply, and I couldn't go in for elaborate and fancy dishes, but then, I didn't want them," he said during an interview that appeared in *Good Housekeeping* magazine in 1903, under the headline, "The Cook Who Sailed Alone."

Cooking on a lamp-stove, Slocum prepared dishes ranging from fish hash and curried venison stew to hot biscuits and doughnuts. Slocum's pantry also included a large amount of hardtack, a coarse cracker that served as a staple for sailors because of its long shelf life. "I used to soak my hardtack and make bread pudding of the very nicest kind," he recalled. The *Spray*'s larder held salt beef and salt pork, but the captain drew much of his protein supply from the sea. "I was in tropical waters most of the time and had flying fish for breakfast pretty much constantly—ah! such breakfasts as I used to have!"

Slocum reached the islands on April 26, 1896—nearly a year to the day after leaving Boston. The island cluster is best known as the one-time home of Alexander Selkirk, a Scottish seaman who, in 1704, was left there alone for four years. Selkirk's story inspired Daniel Defoe's 1719 novel *Robinson Crusoe*. For Slocum, there was "nothing sweeter" than a visit to the cave that once sheltered the real-life Crusoe. He spent his final day at the Juan Fernández Islands walking over green hills, gathering peaches and figs with a group of local Spanish-speaking children who giggled as he spoke to them in English. It was, he later wrote, perhaps the "pleasantest" day of the whole journey.

Leaving Juan Fernández behind, Slocum sailed for an incredible seventy-two days until he reached the Polynesian islands of Samoa—a 5,700-mile, non-stop voyage. His journey across the "vastness" of the Pacific was leisurely, however, particularly compared to his trials in the Strait of Magellan. Were his days spent languishing at the helm, steering the *Spray* for hours on end? Hardly. "I did better than that; for I sat and read my books, mended my clothes, or cooked my meals and ate them in peace," he wrote. "I had already found that it was not good to be alone, and so I made companionship with what there was around me, sometimes with the universe and sometimes with my own insignificant self; but my books were always my friends, let fail all else."

The *Spray*, much to Slocum's delight, was well balanced. That meant she essentially sailed herself, requiring few adjustments of the wheel. Slocum's attention to navigation was just as casual as his attention to the helm. He did not spend hours taking "slavish calculations" to establish his position. Instead, he determined his location "mostly by intuition." Decades at sea gave the captain an understanding of celestial navigation that bordered on a sixth sense. For a full month Slocum sailed across the Pacific with no other guide than the heavens above. "The Southern Cross I saw every night abeam. The sun every morning came up astern; every evening it went down ahead. I wished for no other compass to guide me, for these were true," he wrote.

Samoa marked the second stop on Slocum's literary tour of the Pacific. Anchored in the harbour at Apia, he was greeted by Fanny Stevenson, the recent widow of author Robert Louis Stevenson, one of the captain's literary idols. Slocum toured the author's estate and was invited to pen his letters at Stevenson's

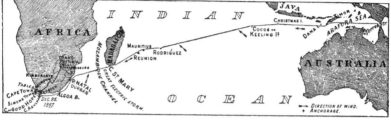

The *Spray*'s course from the Strait of Magellan to Torres Strait, then from Australia to South Africa

desk. As he was throughout much of his journey, Slocum was celebrated at Samoa. Word of his adventure was spreading and many dignitaries and officials were keen to pay tribute to the circumnavigator. At Samoa he dined at the American consulate and called on the local king.

Slocum's arrival was also widely celebrated in Australia. Hailed by a Sydney newspaper as an "enterprising navigator," his solo adventure was described as a journey requiring "a vast amount of courage and determination." But not everyone was pleased to see the captain arrive Down Under. Henry Slater, who readers will remember from Slocum's tumultuous final days aboard the *Northern Light*, was no supporter of his former commander.

Slocum, it will be recalled, put Slater in irons and kept him closely confined for fifty-three days while the *Northern Light* was en route to New York in 1883. The affair tarnished Slocum's reputation, though it did end on a positive note when Slater recanted his damning allegations against the captain. The British ex-convict, now living in Sydney and upset with Slocum's growing fame, denied ever retracting his story. He then recounted for the *Sydney Daily Telegraph* all the allegations of cruelty he first reported in New York. The result was a rehashing of the whole saga just as Slocum was landing in Australia. "I do not make these statements to gain notoriety, or even sympathy, but simply to show my fellow-citizens what kind of a man they are dealing with in Captain Joshua Slocum," Slater said. "You are making a little god of this man, but if I meet him I will make him a little angel."

Such threatening comments quickly landed Slater in court. The affair once again played out in the papers, but this time Slocum appeared to rise above the allegations. The captain offered little comment on Slater's attempt to "blacken" his character. Instead, he handed inquiring reporters a book of newspaper clippings detailing the decade-old affair. Among the clippings was Slater's previous acknowledgement of the captain's innocence. "My whole life," Slocum told a reporter, "is open to inquiry; and I do not think anyone can prove a dishonorable action against me." In the end, the court ordered Slater to pay a bond as surety that he would keep the peace for six months.

In *Sailing Alone*, Slocum offered only a brief and vague allusion to his troubles in Australia and made no mention of Slater. Instead he focused on his months spent relaxing and—occasionally—earning a few dollars. Finding himself low on cash, Slocum charged sixpence for a tour of his boat. "And when this business got dull I caught a shark and charged them sixpence each to look at that," he wrote. It was also in Australia that an admittedly nervous Slocum gave his first paid lecture. "Though I do not feel oppressively lonely on my solitary voyage, I am always glad to get to port," he told a reporter in Australia. "I am, paradoxically as it may seem, really a sociable man."

Slocum spent the winter months of 1897 on Tasmania, the mountainous island south of Australia. "If there was a moment in my voyage when I could have given it up, it was there and then," he wrote. But ever the vagabond, Slocum pushed on. On April 16, 1897—two full years after leaving Boston—he weighed anchor and began making his way up the eastern coast of Australia. "With a good stock of books on board, I fell to reading day and night, leaving this pleasant occupation merely to trim sails or tack, or to lie down and rest, while the *Spray* nibbled at the miles," he wrote.

By June 24, the captain was ready to shove off from Australia and begin his "long voyage" across the Indian Ocean. Arriving at his next desired destination—the Cocos (Keeling) Islands— would again test Slocum's navigational prowess. Located midway between Australia and Sri Lanka, the two coral atolls were 2,700 miles beyond the *Spray*'s bow—two specks off in the vast Indian Ocean. Slocum covered that distance in twenty-three days, during which time he held the *Spray*'s wheel for a mere three hours. "I just lashed the helm and let her go," he wrote. "She always sailed on her course."

Slocum spent a month at the Cocos (Keeling) Islands. On August 20, with the *Spray* tied to a palm tree, he wrote to Joseph B. Gilder, a New York editor who had praised *Voyage of the Liberdade*. The captain was beginning to hatch plans for life after his round-the-world voyage. Among his ideas: taking college students to sea on a "fine sailing ship," where he envisioned teaching them about seafaring and navigation. Not surprisingly, given his previous literary endeavors, Slocum was also eyeing another writing project. "Do you think our people will care for a story of the voyage around?" he asked Gilder.

The *Spray* hauled from the water in Devonport, Tasmania, 1897

While Slocum was sitting under a palm tree, mulling future plans, his family was wondering if he was still alive. "His daughter...has heard nothing from him for some time, and it is believed that his little boat *Spray* has been overcome in an ocean storm," stated an article in the August 24, 1897, edition of the *New Bedford Evening Times*. Many other articles reported Slocum alive, but that was about all they got right. It seems only Slocum himself knew exactly where he had been—and where he was headed.

A report dated September 21 completely bungled Slocum's route, claiming he sailed from Gibraltar to Japan. The report noted the captain was safe, but concluded he had given up his around-the-world attempt. Another article claimed the globe-trotting captain "narrowly escaped being taken by pirates" off the Japanese coast. In Fairhaven, where Slocum rebuilt the *Spray*, a local paper noted that the captain's whereabouts was a topic of conversation "among all who know the brave mariner." That same article, which ran on September 4, 1897, claimed, quite incorrectly, that Slocum and the *Spray* were recently in San Francisco, where they "attracted much attention." The erroneous report went further: Slocum was eyeing an Antarctic voyage. "The captain has long cherished a desire to nail the Stars and Stripes on the South Pole," the paper stated.

Slocum, meanwhile, was hopping between islands in the Indian Ocean. As his family fretted, he was lecturing and enjoying first-rate receptions at tropicals. The error-filled coverage of Slocum's progress is easy to explain. The captain, for reasons unexplained, simply did not write his family much during his voyage—or much at all, for that matter. "Father never wrote a letter to me," Garfield told Walter Teller. Concluded biographer Geoffrey Wolff: "Whether intended or merely feckless, Slocum's silence seems perverse, worse than emotionally stingy."

By December of 1897, Slocum was sailing the *Spray* along the African coast toward the "Cape of Storms." "Christmas off the Cape of Good Hope was passed in a blow that nearly tore the *Spray* to pieces," stated a newspaper report. The captain's leisurely pace continued in nearby Cape Town, where he docked the *Spray* for three full months. He spent the winter of 1898 exploring much of South Africa, aided by a complimentary rail pass.

Perhaps the most peculiar incident of the whole voyage occurred while Slocum was visiting the city of Pretoria. There he met Paul Krüger, the president of the South African Republic (the Transvaal). Slocum was introduced to the president by a judge, who noted the captain was on a voyage "around the world."

Interior—or possibly an exhibit recreation—of the *Spray*'s cabin

"Mr. Krüger corrected the judge rather sharply, reminding him that the world is flat," Slocum wrote. "'You don't mean *round* the world,' said the president; 'it is impossible! You mean *in* the world.'" It was 1898, yet Krüger—or "Uncle Paul," as he was known—still believed the earth was flat. "My friend the judge seemed embarrassed, but I was delighted," Slocum wrote.

In Cape Town, Slocum lectured in front of a packed hall, where, according to one newspaper, "frequent applause rewarded his powers of description." "This success brought me sufficient money for all my needs in port and for the homeward voyage," the captain wrote in *Sailing Alone*. In a letter to his editors, Slocum added: "My ambition is to pay all my little debts before I reach home."

On May 14, off the coast of Brazil, the captain spied the *Oregon*, an American battleship. The *Oregon*'s captain signalled Slocum, asking if he had seen any warships about. Unbeknownst to Slocum, the Spanish-American War was underway and he was sailing through hostile waters. Unfazed, he signalled back—informing his fellow captain that, no, he had not seen any Spanish warships. Slocum, exhibiting his sense of humour, then added: "Let us keep together for mutual protection." The *Oregon*, a thousand times the size of the *Spray*, offered no further response and steamed off in hunt of the enemy.

A cartoon printed in the *Cape Town Owl* of March 5, 1898, in connection with Slocum's trip to Pretoria and his visit with Paul Krüger, the president of the South African Republic

Following quick stops in the West Indies, the *Spray* was "booming joyously along for home." After enduring a "furious" hail and lightning storm off New York, Slocum guided his sloop toward Newport, Rhode Island. At one o'clock in the morning on June 27, 1898, as the residents of Newport slept, Slocum dropped anchor in the harbour. The great voyage, which covered forty-six thousand miles and spanned more than three years, was over.

Wrote Slocum: "No king, no country, no treasury at all, was taxed for the voyage of the *Spray*, and she accomplished all that she undertook to do."

CHAPTER 7

LOST ON LAND

Rising from his bunk on the morning of June 27, 1898, Slocum awoke to an America noticeably different from the one he departed three years earlier. For starters, the country was at war, a fact made obvious to him the night before as he guided the *Spray* past mines in Newport Harbor.

The 1898 conflict between the US and Spain grew out of American sympathy for Cuban rebels seeking independence from Spain. Calls for American intervention escalated—and were realized—after the mysterious sinking of the USS *Maine* battleship in Havana Harbor. The war, which was entirely one-sided, ended Spanish colonial rule in the Americas. The victorious Americans, meanwhile, earned new territories and world power status. The conflict also robbed Slocum of his headlines. Celebrated and honoured abroad, the captain returned home to a tepid welcome.

The *Newport Herald* reported Slocum's arrival on page three of its June 28 edition, noting a small craft had "swung lazily into the harbor." "She was a stranger in these waters," the paper noted. The *Boston Globe*'s report was located on page twelve, though it was more encouraging, noting the *Spray* and her "gallant skipper" received "hundreds" of visitors. The *New York Herald*, on page nine, reported that Slocum sent a telegram

"The Crew at Breakfast": Slocum standing in the companionway of the *Spray* in 1902. Photograph by Clifton Johnson.

Slocum at his farm on Martha's Vineyard, with Hettie in the doorway, 1902

to his wife on the morning of his arrival. Hettie arrived at Newport that evening. "As she had three times mourned her husband as dead their reunion was touching," the paper noted. Clearly Slocum's three-year absence was not easy on Hettie.

In *Sailing Alone*, Slocum wrote that he "profited in many ways by the voyage." "As for aging, why, the dial of my life was turned back till my friends all said, 'Slocum is young again,'" he wrote. And the *Spray*? "She was still as sound as a nut, and as tight as the best ship afloat. She did not leak a drop—not one drop!" he boasted. Shortly after his arrival, Slocum received a telegram from Richard Watson Gilder, editor of the prestigious *Century Illustrated Monthly Magazine*. Gilder was curious: was the captain interested in writing about his voyage? Slocum, not surprisingly, jumped at the offer. In a June 30 letter to Gilder, he admitted his lack of experience in magazine writing but pledged to enter into the assignment with "a great deal of energy."

Slocum's letter to Gilder also reveals disappointment at the level of attention his journey was generating on home shores. "When my countrymen come to know about it and have time to think it over they will not be ashamed of the *Spray*," he wrote. "I know that the whole story will be hard to beat." In a second letter to Gilder, Slocum dismissed a rumour claiming he smuggled diamonds in from South Africa. There were no diamonds aboard the *Spray*, he insisted, only gold—"enough to pay the old debts I made when I owned and sailed the bigger ship." He also felt the need to again defend the significance of his overshadowed journey. "Have any of your merchant captains accomplished more—with such limited resources?" he asked. And though only back on shore a matter of days, Slocum was quickly consumed by the feelings of idleness that plagued him at the journey's start. With a war raging, he longed to make a contribution. "I burn to be of some use now," he wrote in a letter published in the *New Bedford Standard* on July 3, 1898. "There is some life still in the old man."

A week after landing in Newport, Slocum sailed the *Spray* to Fairhaven. He anchored off Poverty Point, not far from where the sloop was rebuilt. A local newspaper, familiar with Slocum and his travels, was more generous in its praise of the journey. "Captain Slocum has arrived from the most remarkable voyage ever attempted by any navigator," the paper stated. Stepping on board, the reporter found the *Spray*'s cabin full of "curiosities"—including shells and a large bamboo stick given to him by the widow of Robert Louis Stevenson. Slocum told the reporter he planned to "get a little rest" in Fairhaven. "I intend to remain around here a few days and will then go cruising with my wife and son," he told the paper. "I intend to go to London before long."

That plan, like many of those developed in the years after his famous voyage, did not materialize. For instance, he again floated the idea of running a "college ship." The clipper ship, he proposed, would carry three hundred students on a two-year cruise around the world. Courses would range from navigation to the liberal arts, and Slocum planned to teach nautical astronomy. Despite his enthusiasm, the plan did not progress any further.

As he did at various ports along his route, Slocum lectured often about his adventures. Those talks—which took place frequently in halls, theatres, and yacht clubs around New England—provided the captain with the bulk of his income in the years immediately following his return. His talks covered the highlights of his voyage and were illustrated by lantern slides made from photographs he took along the way. An advertisement for a December 1899 Slocum lecture hailed his trip as "the most remarkable voyage of modern times." Outside of lecturing, however, the captain discovered his prospects were again limited. "A genius at navigation, dead reckoning, calculating lunar tables, and surviving tempests, he was frequently lost on land," concluded author Geoffrey Wolff. With his other plans failing to launch, Slocum set out to put his adventures to paper.

Though he clearly enjoyed writing, the captain regularly questioned his ability. Slocum was confident at the helm of a ship, but less so when holding a pen. "I don't know how to apologize sufficiently for the stupidity of my undisciplined hand," he wrote to his editors in October 1894, referring to errors he made in writing *Voyage of the Liberdade*. Such sentiments continued during the writing and editing process for *Sailing Alone*. "I am glad that my poor manuscript fell into good hands," he wrote in an 1899 letter to Clarence Buel, assistant editor at *Century Illustrated Monthly Magazine*. "How patient Century Editors have been! I appreciate every touch of the pen given to my poor story."

Captain Slocum's Lectures.

INCIDENTS AND EVENTS

WHILE

CIRCUMNAVIGATING THE GLOBE ALONE

IN THE

Yacht "SPRAY."

Illustrated by Lantern Views.

. . . PRESS COMMENTS. . . .

"The Captain is an excellent reconteur; he kept a crowded house in a state of highest amusement."—THE OWL (Cape Town). *Doctor Gill Astronomer Royal Chairman*

"At the Bree Street Congregational Church . . . a most interesting account of his voyage in his self-built boat . . . most entertaining . . . beautiful limelight views."—STANDARD AND DIGGERS' NEWS. *Burgomaster Chairman*

"A pleasant style and much natural humor, which took immensely with the audience."—DIAMOND FIELDS' ADVERTISER.

"The placard rarely exhibited in Cape Town "House Full" had to be put up early in the evening . . . a large attendance of ladies. In humorous vein the Captain traced his lonely voyage through all the climes he had visited; frequent applause rewarding his powers of description."—THE CAPE ARGUS.

"The Captain's graphic and humorous style held the absorbed attention of his listeners throughout."—THE CAPE TIMES.

Had to do something for expenses of the voyage. Other captains might draw bottomary bonds but I lectured the Spray around the world. J. S.

An advertisement for a Slocum lecture

The first installment of Slocum's story appeared in *Century Illustrated* in September 1899. The episodes ran each month until March 1900. In November 1899, *The New York Times* (which failed to report Slocum's arrival home a year earlier) needled the captain in its "Topics of the Times" column. Specifically, the

The *Spray*: "Splendid Ship" or "Damned Bucket"?

As Walter Teller noted, the *Spray* remained a "controversial subject" for some time. Tracking abilities aside, some questioned her stability and seaworthiness. The harshest critic was Howard Chapelle, a curator at the Smithsonian Institute. "She was not an ideal vessel for long ocean voyages—unless Slocum was aboard," he wrote in April 1965, claiming the *Spray* was "badly framed and fastened." "It is sheer ignorance to tout this damned bucket as a 'splendid ship'…. The old man was a prime seaman to stay on top, with her, as long as he did." Kenneth Slack, of Australia, dedicated an entire book to the study of Slocum's vessel, *In the Wake of the Spray*. His conclusion: the performance of the *Spray* under Slocum—and the performance of later copies sailed by far less skilled sailors—was more than enough to prove her seafaring ability. "For those who want a sturdy vessel of proven seaworthiness, safe, able and fast for ocean work—the *Spray* design has a lot to recommend," he wrote.

article questioned the *Spray*'s self-steering ability. Did Slocum really lash the helm and let his ship do the rest? "The tale is painfully hard to believe," stated the anonymous columnist. Slocum's retort was published in the *Times* on November 11, but still the columnist continued to pursue the issue. In an 1899 letter to Buel, the captain concluded the matter with this line: "The *Times* joker I can stow any time in my waistcoat pocket."

Slocum's enduring work, *Sailing Alone Around the World*, was published in its entirety by the Century Company in the spring of 1900. The 294-page volume included illustrations and a cover decorated with an anchor and two seahorses. Slocum, already insecure about his writing—and generally sensitive to criticism—waited anxiously for the reviews to come in. "I have heard nothing from the critics about my 'fine writing' and hope to hear nothing," he wrote to his editor on May 4, 1900. "If they'll only pass me this time I'll steer clear…in the future."

The *Spray* at Port Antonio, Jamaica

The captain's anxiety was misplaced, however. "His voyage was interesting; his book is better," stated a review in the *Nautical Gazette*. "There is no question as to his name being handed down to posterity as one of the most intrepid of navigators." British journalist and author Sir Edwin Arnold echoed that sentiment, calling *Sailing Alone* "the most extraordinary book, in its way, ever published." "The adventure itself is by far the most courageous, sustained and successful enterprise of the kind ever undertaken by mortal man," he added. A review in *The Nation* called Slocum a "valiant and resourceful man," while noting he was "a type of American seaman that…is passing out of existence."

Originally priced at two dollars, the book sold about seven thousand copies in its first year. It has since established itself as a classic. Still in print, Slocum's book—and his storytelling style—has proven popular across generations. According to Geoffrey Wolff, more than fifty thousand copies of *Sailing Alone* have been

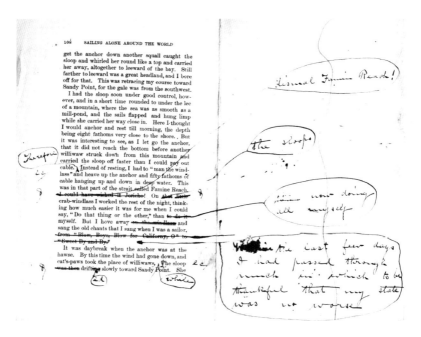

Changes made by Slocum to a draft of *Sailing Alone Around the World*

sold in its various editions and translations. More than a century after its release, *Sailing Alone* is still a pleasure to read. A modern reader cannot help but be struck by Slocum's seafaring skill, as well as by his ability to weave a salty tale. "The wonder is that a man with such a limited boyhood education, and who had been knocking about the sea nearly ever since, should be able to turn to authorship and express himself so forcibly and fluently," noted one writer.

His publishing efforts were proven successful, but the captain continued to struggle in developing other ventures. In late 1899, in a letter to Clarence Buel, his editor, Slocum wrote of his desire to sail to Iceland. Yet only a few months later, in March 1900, Slocum was on to another plan: he would sell his prized *Spray* to buy a new vessel. "People buy things rare in history.

Someone may buy my old boat and so help me into my submarine explorer," he wrote. It's not clear what vessel Slocum was referring to. Regardless, the plan did not materialize. Then, in February 1901, the restless captain wrote of his desire to serve as a second mate on a "flying ship." "I am not the old fossil that some take me for and I am not for old ideas when new are better," he wrote.

Slocum lived something of a vagabond existence in the years after his arrival home. He spent much of his time aboard the *Spray*, particularly as he visited and lectured at ports in New England. He also spent some time in East Boston, living with Hettie's sisters. During the winter of 1900, Slocum and Hettie shared an apartment in New York while his son, Garfield, stayed nearby on the *Spray*. "Father did not come onboard the *Spray* much, did not come to inquire if I needed any food or if he could help me; was a mystery to me and will be to my dying day," Garfield wrote in a letter to Walter Teller.

Then, one day, Slocum appeared with news. They were headed upstate to Buffalo for the Pan-American Exposition.

The cover of a first-edition *Sailing Alone Around the World*

Held between May and November of 1901, the fair included everything from dancing native tribes to wild animal shows to a re-enactment of Custer's Last Stand. The event took place at an expansive site in northwestern New York, which included a large lake. It was there that Slocum was paid to display the *Spray*. The assignment required navigating the sloop inland along the Erie Canal, which connects New York City to the Great Lakes. Slocum bought a small gas engine and attached it to a "clinker" lifeboat. With Garfield at the controls, this rickety vessel towed the *Spray* (with Slocum and Hettie onboard) toward Buffalo.

At the exposition grounds, visitors were charged admission to go on board and meet the "gallant captain." Garfield reported that many visitors called on the *Spray*, including US President William McKinley, who was later assassinated at the exposition. That episode aside, the exposition proved a success for Slocum. He made extra cash by selling his books as well as souvenir booklets. The thin booklets, arranged by Hettie, were simply a collection of articles written about his round-the-world voyage. But there was one unique feature: each pamphlet contained a small piece of the *Spray* mainsail that was destroyed near Cape Horn.

The money generated from the Buffalo trip helped the struggling captain fund his next venture: a farm on Martha's Vineyard, the Massachusetts island located off Cape Cod. When the exposition ended, Slocum was alone. Garfield was off at another job, and Hettie had already retreated to Martha's Vineyard. The makeshift tugboat was also gone, so a horse towed the *Spray* back to New York. "With an old work horse for a sail, the *Spray* sailed down the Erie Canal yesterday afternoon," a newspaper reported. Despite their time together on the *Spray*, Slocum and Garfield were not particularly close. "I wonder how father steered the horse on his return; he did not write to me and tell me about his return trip," the captain's son told Walter Teller.

From New York the captain headed to Martha's Vineyard to try his hand at farming. "The hand that steered the tiller of the *Spray* will steer the plow," a newspaper noted. "He intends to be a farmer, and only use the *Spray* for small trips on business."

In the summer of 1902, Slocum received a letter from Clifton Johnson. The Massachusetts writer and photographer wanted to visit and interview the captain at his new home in West Tisbury, a community on Martha's Vineyard. Slocum enthusiastically agreed. So Johnson visited the farm where Slocum, the sailor-turned-landsman, had "cast anchor." "He lives on the outskirts of a rural village with several old sea captains for neighbors," Johnson wrote in *Outing* magazine in October 1902. "His house is one of the most ancient on the island—an oak-ribbed ark of a dwelling with warped floors and tiny window panes and open fireplaces. Its aspect is at present rather forlorn and naked, but the captain knows how to wield the hammer and the saw, and will soon make it snug."

A newspaper clipping describing Slocum's trip from the Pan-American Exposition in Buffalo to his new home on Martha's Vineyard

Garfield told Walter Teller that his father bought the small house because its timbers reminded him of the hold of a ship. A man of the world, Slocum added new roofing that resembled a Japanese temple. Shells and chunks of coral sat beside the door. The original plan, Garfield wrote, was to raise fruit trees. "In a single season he has become an enthusiastic agriculturalist [and] is proud of his flourishing garden," Johnson wrote in his profile. "Martha's Vineyard looks to him like Eden, and it seems likely the sea will know him no more."

That assessment was premature. The captain tried his hand at growing fruit and hops, but he was no farmer. Slocum, to his core, was a sailor. In one of this letters to Johnson he referred to the farm jokingly as "Rudder Ranch." But Hettie told Teller her husband called the farm "Fag End"—referring to the useless end of a rope. With his farming efforts proving less than fruitful (and his lecturing career fading) Slocum eventually strayed back to the water and his beloved sloop. "I think there was some trouble in the house, so he returned to the sea," Garfield told Teller. "I assume that he and Hettie did not pull on the same rope." Added Garfield: "Father was a changed man on his return from his lonely voyage—he acted to me as though he wanted to be alone. That voyage was a terrible strain on him."

George Gifford, the long-time storekeeper in West Tisbury, told Teller that it was general opinion that Slocum and Hettie had separated. "Nothing legal," Gifford noted, "just that he went his way and she went hers." (In the summer of 1908, the *Vineyard Gazette*, likely in jest, reported Slocum as a "recent guest of Mrs. Slocum at West Tisbury.") Slocum's strained connection with Hettie was mirrored in other relationships. He was reportedly prone to quarrelling with his brother, Ornan, who ran a shoe shop on Martha's Vineyard. In his unpublished notes, Clifton Johnson wrote that Slocum "has a temper and explodes like a firecracker when he is affronted." It would appear that Slocum's affections were reserved for his oldest son. "My son Victor—just home from a whaling voyage—is helping me repair the shack," he wrote to Johnson in September 1902. "He is quite a sailor."

Captain Slocum in his later years

CHAPTER 8

ON THE
OUTGOING TIDE

FROM 1903 TO 1908, Slocum spent much of his time on the *Spray*. In the winter months he often sailed south to avoid the cold. During the warmer months he sailed along the New England coast, mainly around Martha's Vineyard. He gave the odd talk and sold the shells he collected down south. In November of 1905, Slocum left Martha's Vineyard for his annual respite in southern waters, which included stops at ports in Cuba and Jamaica. In early April 1906, after a leisurely two months spent collecting shells at Grand Cayman, Slocum headed north again. His cargo included about a thousand shells, as well as a dozen rare orchids, which the captain was asked to deliver to none other than the president, Theodore Roosevelt. That important delivery was delayed, however, after Slocum drifted into some surprising and serious legal trouble.

By Thursday, May 24, the *Spray* was tied up at Riverton, New Jersey. That night, Slocum gave a lecture at the Riverton Yacht Club. The following day he welcomed visitors aboard the *Spray*, including twelve-year-old Elsie Wright, who toured the sloop in the afternoon with a friend. On Friday evening, after his visitors had gone, Slocum called on Leslie Miller, a friend who summered at Martha's Vineyard. "Slocum was lean and hungry looking and gaunt," recalled Miller's son, Percy. "There was no mistaking he was an old sea dog." The captain listened to Percy play the piano before heading back to the *Spray*. At nine o'clock, while stepping off a trolley car,

Slocum was arrested and charged with raping Elsie Wright.

The allegations against Slocum were outlined in a number of newspaper reports. "CAPT. SLOCUM IN TROUBLE," stated a headline in the *Riverton New Era*. The article said the alleged incident took place while Wright and her young male friend were visiting the *Spray* Friday afternoon. "It is said that while the boy was on deck the skipper showed the little girl through the cabin, and then the assault is alleged to have occurred," the paper stated.

Slocum in an undated photograph

"His arrest came as a startling surprise after a round of entertainments in his honor," another paper noted. "The old sailor was indignant at his arrest. He ridiculed the charge against him, and when being taken to the jail said he would be vindicated." Added another report: "Capt. Slocum said he had no recollection of the misdemeanor with which he is charged, and if it occurred it must have been during one of the mental lapses to which he was subject." Bail was set at one thousand dollars. Unable to afford such a sum, Slocum sat in jail for forty-two days. On July 6, the matter was put before a judge and the captain did not contest a lesser charge of indecent assault. "I am very sorry to be obliged to administer reproof to a man of your experience and years," stated the judge.

"Upon request of the family I can deal leniently with you." Slocum was discharged and told to never return to Riverton by rail or water.

Exactly what happened that day on the *Spray* is unclear. It is apparent, however, that Slocum did not rape Wright. At one point the girl's father wrote a letter to the *Riverton New Era*, emphasizing that no physical injury had occurred. A doctor, called by Wright's parents, concluded, "she was not much injured, but was suffering from shock." In the end, the alleged incident was downgraded to a "great indiscretion." So what happened? "Was his fly undone, intentionally or carelessly? Did he say something obscene to her?" wondered Geoffrey Wolff in his analysis of the event. "I can imagine a young girl recoiling from a grizzled, bald, and bewhiskered old man with wrinkles, liver spots, an arthritic claw of a hand, bad breath, and a few missing teeth," he concluded.

Regardless of what actually happened, one must assume from Slocum's next stop that his reputation had not suffered. From Riverton, free of the allegations and embarrassment that had dogged him for weeks, the captain sailed north to Oyster Bay, New York. The reason for his August visit: to deliver the one surviving orchid to Teddy Roosevelt.

Archibald Roosevelt, one of the president's sons, was sailing around Oyster Bay in a small boat when he spied the *Spray*. Slocum, now in his sixties, invited Archie aboard. An avid sailor, Archie was greatly entertained by the old captain's "yarns." That evening, the boy reported the visit to his father. Roosevelt enthusiastically told his son to invite the captain up to Sagamore Hill, the president's nearby summer house. As Walter Teller succinctly concluded: "Slocum had navigated in a matter of days from a cell in a Jersey jail to a place as guest of the president." After meeting Roosevelt, Slocum took Archie and a sailor from the president's yacht on a cruise from Oyster Bay to Newport, Rhode Island.

Slocum entertaining visitors in Oyster Bay

"It was a marvelous adventure for a child," Archie wrote years later, recalling meals of salt fish and enormous pancakes "as thick as your foot."

Slocum's visit with the Roosevelts must have filled the aging captain with a feeling of vindication following his stint in jail. It also appeared to inspire his next unsuccessful plan. By mid-September of 1906 the *Spray* was docked at a New Bedford wharf and Slocum was talking about a trip through the Panama Canal, then under construction. "It is not my wish to be the first to go through the Panama Canal," he told a local paper. "The logical man for that honor will be President Roosevelt...on the best battleship in our navy." After the president's entourage, Slocum added, the *Spray* would follow. Slocum disappeared before the canal opened in 1914. But he did meet again with Roosevelt.

In the spring of 1907, Slocum departed the Cayman Islands bound for Martha's Vineyard. The *Spray*'s deck, the *New York World* reported, was piled high with souvenirs for selling in northern waters, including "forest orchids, strange coral and other wonders of the South seas." In May, the New England-bound skipper sailed up the Potomac River and anchored at the foot of Seventh Street in Washington. Archie Roosevelt greeted him at the dock. "Father wants to see you," said Archie, standing with his dog, Skip. From the dock Slocum was taken to the White House by wagon. "They made me wait in what they called the red room. Pretty soon the President came in and we had a long chat," the captain recalled. Among Roosevelt's questions for Slocum: would he again visit Oyster Bay and take Archie out for another trip in the *Spray*? Clearly Roosevelt was not concerned about the captain's previous legal troubles.

On July 13, the "kindly old" captain sailed his "weather-beaten" vessel into the bay near the president's summer home. "He comes to Oyster Bay for just one purpose—to see his chum, Archie Roosevelt," the *New York World* reported. "Archie is learning the art of sailing from the old sea dog." Despite his faded prospects, Slocum was still capable of drawing a crowd. "Everybody in the village has rowed out to shake hands with the captain," the newspaper reported. "They have come to look upon him as one of the wonders of the deep."

Walter Teller put a tremendous amount of effort into filling the biographical gaps in Slocum's life. Much of Teller's work fleshed out Slocum's final years—a period highlighted by the decline of both the captain and his sloop. Simply put, both Slocum and the *Spray* were breaking down.

Vincent Gilpin, an author and yachtsman, saw the aging captain in Miami in January 1908. Gilpin attended a Slocum lecture at a local school auditorium and later visited the captain

The Captain's Famous Fish Chowder

Slocum aboard the *Spray* in Washington, DC, 1907

Joshua Slocum was not a boastful man. But there was one area where he felt his skills exceeded those of the average man: the art of making fish chowder.

"My friends…often ask me to make a chowder for them; and when I do…it brings them right to their feet," he told *Good Housekeeping* magazine in 1903. Here, in his own words, is Slocum's technique for making cod chowder: "Put some pork and a sliced onion in the pot and let that cook awhile. Then put in a layer of potatoes and next a layer of fish, and so on up to the top with a seasoning of salt and pepper. Then add enough water to barely cover it and cook for twenty minutes. When it is about done put in milk and bits of cracker or bread and let it simmer a little."

aboard the *Spray*. "He was thrifty and usually hard up—which didn't bother him, for his wants were few," Gilpin wrote in a letter to Teller. "The *Spray* was very simply fitted out, rather bare, and very damp…I remember seeing him lunching one day on what looked like a half-baked potato, from which he sliced pieces with his jackknife. He was rather shabbily dressed in civilian clothes, with a ragged black felt hat," Gilpin continued in his 1956 letter. "On the whole, I thought him a good example of the old-line Yankee skipper, competent, self-reliant, not talkative, but perfectly friendly and ready to answer questions…A very capable man; and a lonely, unhappy man."

Ernest Dean, a friend from Martha's Vineyard, was working as a yacht captain in the Bahamas when he ran into Slocum in 1908. Dean attended the captain's lecture in Nassau. Some time later he saw Slocum on a wharf with a group of local men, one of whom was holding a cloth over his bleeding mouth. A rattled Slocum told Dean the group of men—"ginned up some"—had been speaking poorly of the *Spray*. Apparently one of the men labelled Slocum a liar for claiming he sailed around the world in such a small boat. "I looked up in time to see which one said it, made a leap, and with a couple of side-winders, unshipped his jaw," Slocum told Dean, again displaying his thin skin. How did Dean sum up Slocum's decline? "When I first met him and the *Spray* they both were neat, trim and seaworthy, but as the years rolled along I noticed…signs of wear and exposure."

Louise Ward, an American reporter, met Slocum in Kingston, Jamaica, during this period. The *Spray*, she recalled, appeared old. The captain, meanwhile, seemed "rather sad." "I remember he said to me: 'I can patch up the *Spray* but who will patch up Captain Slocum?'"

The deteriorating state of the captain and his boat is perhaps best revealed in the recollections of H. S. Smith. In his twenties, Smith and three sailing buddies sought out the famed captain after being told Slocum was back in Fairhaven. The four young men found the *Spray* floating in a creek on the Fairhaven side of the Acushnet River. Slocum sat slumped by the wheel, looking dejected in the hot sun. The captain, Smith recalled in a letter to Teller, resembled "a typical beachcomber": "He wore a battered old felt hat…unbuttoned trousers that would disgrace a clam-digger and a pair of high lace-up shoes badly in need of a polish."

Hailing the captain, they asked to come aboard. "Yes," Slocum replied. "But it will cost you boys ten cents apiece." After a search

of their pockets the young men produced forty cents and stepped on deck. "The little ship was filthy and almost everything aboard was dilapidated," Smith recalled in an article in the March 1968 edition of *The Skipper*, a yachting magazine. "Captain Slocum himself answered our questions in a slow and hesitating way, indicating a kind of mental slothfulness or perhaps senility." Smith also recalled vividly the captain's many conch shells, all in a "putrefying condition." "I can still remember that smell," he wrote. "The odor permeated the whole ship and added to the general atmosphere of dirt, neglect and decay."

Slocum on the *Spray* in 1907. Both the captain and his ship had seen better days.

Much to their delight, however, Slocum allowed the four men to help him sail the *Spray* to New Bedford for supplies.

"So all hands got to work, directed by Slocum, who stayed by the wheel and gave his orders in a very crisp, sharp fashion without shouting—a far cry from his earlier hesitant mumbling," Smith noted of Slocum's transformation from a dozy old man to an energetic sea captain. Slocum eventually handed Smith the wheel. "But there was little steering to be done. She held her course perfectly, with hardly a touch on the wheel." At New Bedford, Slocum went on shore while Smith and his crew further explored the *Spray*. "But everywhere we looked, we encountered dirt, shoddy workmanship, decay—and the ever present stench of tired conch," he wrote. "It was depressing."

Simply put, Slocum's prized vessel was in rough condition. The captain had resurrected the old sloop—and, in turn, his own prospects—more than a decade earlier. But now both man and ship were deteriorating. "From what we saw that afternoon, there is no question in my mind that the *Spray* was a slow, docile, seakindly craft that would take care of herself for days at a time," Smith noted, "but the shape she was in would give horrors to anyone who went to sea."

Some time later, Slocum set off in his sloop from Martha's Vineyard. The sixty-four-year-old captain told friends and acquaintances that he planned to sail to Venezuela and head up the Orinoco River to the headwaters of the Amazon. He was never seen again.

Two mysteries surround Slocum's disappearance. The first concerns the year he actually went missing. Many sources cite November 14, 1909, as the day he departed Martha's Vineyard for the last time. That was the date Hettie wrote on a court document in 1912. But as Ann Spencer detailed in her Slocum biography, *Alone at Sea*, numerous newspaper articles reported that Slocum vanished in November of 1908, not 1909. For instance, a July 24, 1910, article in the *New Bedford Sunday Standard* reported that

A newspaper clipping announcing Slocum's disappearance at sea

the "fearless navigator" departed in November 1908, headed south to the West Indies for the winter. The article noted the captain was spotted in a gale a few days out of Martha's Vineyard. Nothing had been heard from the captain since; no other sightings were reported and no wreckage was spotted. "[Slocum] is probably now resting at the bottom of the ocean," the paper concluded. "I should as soon expect to see the dead rise as I should to see Captain Slocum," Hettie told the paper. "He is lost in all probability, probably run down by a steamer at night."

Hettie's theorizing brings us to the second mystery: what happened to Slocum? Did the weathered *Spray* finally throw a plank or succumb to rough seas? Or did the aging skipper suffer a heart attack, stroke, or simply get washed overboard? Like Hettie, Victor Slocum concluded a steamship likely cut down his father at night. Garfield told Teller his father longed for a burial at sea. "And he got his wish."

Or, did Slocum—who grew increasingly reclusive in his later years—simply decide to cut off all communication with his friends and family in New England? On May 27, 1911, the *New Bedford Evening Standard* reported the sighting of a "lone

His favourite perch: Slocum standing on the *Spray*'s bowsprit, 1902

mariner" on the Orinoco River. "WHITE MAN SEEN ON THE ORINOCO RIVER MAY BE CAPTAIN JOSHUA SLOCUM," stated the headline. The report was based on nothing more than rumours in the shipping community, but it offered a "dim ray of hope" that Slocum was safe, nearly three years after departing Martha's Vineyard. "There is yet the chance that the captain may return in the *Spray*," the paper stated.

That is a comforting way to picture Slocum's final years: sailing his trusted sloop, exploring foreign ports, savouring his "solitude supreme," and embracing— not fearing—the rigours of life at sea. "To face the elements is, to be sure, no light matter when the sea is in its grandest mood," he wrote in *Sailing Alone*. "But where, after all, would be the poetry of the sea were there no wild waves?"

The Slocum monument on Brier Island. Located near the Westport waterfront, the bronze plaque was unveiled in 1961.

FADING INTO THE FOG

BRIER ISLAND IS shrouded in fog as Robert Hersey sets to work. After dipping a brush into a bucket of soapy water, he begins scrubbing dirt and seagull droppings off a bronze plaque.

Unveiled on July 22, 1961, the weathered plate is part of a small monument honouring the island's most famous former resident, Joshua Slocum—"The first man to sail around the world alone." The bronze tablet, which sits atop a cairn made of beach stones, offers a few lines of biographical information and etchings of the captain and his sloop, the *Spray*.

The view from the monument has changed little from the days when a young Slocum walked to this point by the water's edge, a short stroll from the Westport waterfront. A strong tide is ripping past nearby rocks and the caw of gulls fills the air.

Both the plaque and cairn have seen better days. The plaque is tarnished and dirty; the mortar holding the cairn together is worn and cracking. "This monument sees some pretty hard nor'easters in the wintertime—driving wind and salt," Hersey says as he scrubs vigorously. Hersey, a program coordinator and heritage advisor with the Municipality of Digby, has travelled to the island on this day for one reason: to clean and patch up the "neglected" Slocum monument.

Slocum's memory, like the Brier Island cairn constructed to honour him, has faded in recent decades. Many of the organizations and memorials established to honour the captain have

In 1987 the Territory of Christmas Island issued a "Famous Visitors" stamp depicting Slocum. The captain sighted the island on July 11, 1897, while sailing in the Indian Ocean.

either disappeared or fallen from view. The high-water mark of Slocum memorializing occurred between 1955–65. In 1955, sailing enthusiast Richard Gordon McCloskey founded the Joshua Slocum Society International. The non-profit organization had three goals: to encourage long distance passages in small boats; to recognize acts of heroism at sea; and to keep alive the "memory and legacy" of the famous captain for which it was named. The society's membership included boat builders, circumnavigators, Slocum descendants, and sailors of large and small boats alike. At its height, the society boasted members in twenty-five countries. It also issued a journal, fittingly called *The Spray*. In June 1998, the group helped promote ceremonies celebrating the centennial of Slocum's round-the-world voyage.

On Brier Island, Slocum Society members oversaw the maintenance of the local memorial. But in July 2011, with participation waning, the international society disbanded. With it died the network of Slocum enthusiasts dedicated to preserving his memory and maintaining the monuments built in his honour. "There was nobody left," Hersey says of his efforts to find a guardian for the Brier Island monument. "I couldn't find anybody to do it."

The first significant Slocum memorial was

Slocum memorial plaque in Fairhaven, Massachusetts

dedicated in April of 1959. A bronze plaque (nearly identical to the one later placed at Brier Island) was fixed to a large boulder at Poverty Point, the site in Fairhaven where Slocum rebuilt the *Spray*. "Modern-day man would do well to follow the example of individuality and courage exemplified by Captain Joshua Slocum," biographer Walter Teller told the crowd assembled. The monument sits on the edge of a small, grassy lot, facing onto the Acushnet River and the New Bedford waterfront—the same view Slocum enjoyed while sawing and nailing planks in the early 1890s.

This tombstone marks the Westport grave of Slocum's mother, Sarah Jane

In July 1965, another bronze plaque was affixed to a small boulder and placed outside the house Slocum once owned in West Tisbury on Martha's Vineyard. Forty-five people attended the dedication ceremony, including ten people who knew Slocum personally. Today the plaque is surrounded on three sides by a weathered wooden fence and goes unnoticed by the majority of drivers passing by the captain's old farmhouse.

Many of the key sites from Slocum's early life are also tucked away—recognized as historically significant, but largely uncelebrated. On Brier Island, the old cobbler shop where a young Slocum endured his dreaded days making leather boots remains perched on the edge of Westport Harbour. Previously used as a storage shed by local fishermen, the heritage property is now painted bright red and houses a gift shop. In a nearby cemetery, on a hill above the Westport waterfront, a weathered and cracked gravestone marks the resting place of Slocum's mother, Sarah Jane. On this particular day, a small glass spice jar rests at the base of the grave marker. Inside is a damp, ink-stained note. Addressed to "Sarah Slocum," it reads: "Thanks for having a son that has inspired thousands to take up tools to rebuild or build boats from scratch. And to fulfill their dreams of far away lands…." Five captains, including one building a *Spray* replica, signed and quietly placed the note at the grave.

Not far from the cemetery stands the Westport Baptist Church—"the little church on the hill," as Slocum described it in *Sailing Alone*. As a boy Slocum sat in pew thirteen, the bench frequented by members of his mother's family. In the 1970s, an old piece of the pew was found in the church attic. On October 14, 1973, the panel—still marked with the number thirteen—was restored, attached to the church wall, and dedicated to the island's most famous son. Affixed to the panel is a plaque engraved with a poem. The verse was found in one of the oldest homes on Brier Island, tucked in a leather-bound book of psalms.

> Not in the churchyard shall he sleep,
> Amid the silent gloom;
> His home was on the mighty deep,
> And there shall be his tomb.
>
> He loved his own bright, deep-blue sea;
> O'er it he loved to roam;
> And now his winding sheet shall be
> That same bright ocean's foam.
>
> No village bell shall toll for him
> Its mournful, solemn dirge;
> The winds shall chant a requiem
> To him beneath the surge.

ACKNOWLEDGEMENTS

I owe thanks to the many people who aided my work on this project. Their contributions span the entire process, from the initial planning to the final edits. They are: Peter Moreira and Jacques Poitras, trusted colleagues who offered key advice before I started out; my good friend Ben Shingler, for his thoughtful recommendations to my initial draft; Rob Hersey and Laura Titus for aiding my research on Brier Island; Hannah Beecher, who showed me around Slocum's former home on Martha's Vineyard; Michael Dyer, Melanie Correia, Mark Procknik, Michael Lapides, and Jan Keeler at the New Bedford Whaling Museum; Debbie Charpentier and (document scanner extraordinaire) Suzanne Kowal at the Millicent Library in Fairhaven; Dana Constanza Street and Catherine Mayhew at the Martha's Vineyard Museum; Christopher Richard at the Fairhaven Office of Tourism; Jamie Serran at the Yarmouth County Museum and Archives; my excellent editors at Nimbus: Patrick Murphy for his enthusiasm and guidance and Whitney Moran for her attentive editing and many superb suggestions; my brother, Tom, who first insisted I read *Sailing Alone Around the World*; and, of course, my wife, Eva Barkova, for all her support and encouragement, even while she was working on a far more difficult project.

Thank you, all.

BIBLIOGRAPHY

Druett, Joan. *Hen Frigates: Wives of Merchant Captains Under Sail*. New York: Simon & Schuster, 1998.

Hugo, David T. "Nova Scotia to Martha's Vineyard: Notes on Captain Joshua Slocum." *The Dukes County Intelligencer*, August 1969, 3–22.

Johnson, Clifton. "Captain Joshua Slocum: The Man Who Sailed Alone Around the World in a Thirty-seven-Foot Boat." *Tales of Old New England*, ed. Frank Oppel. Castle Books, 1987.

Slack, Kenneth E. *In the Wake of the "Spray."* New Brunswick, New Jersey: Rutgers University Press, 1966.

Slocum, Joshua. *The Annotated Sailing Alone Around the World*, ed. Rod Scher. Dobbs Ferry, New York: Sheridan House, 2009.

———. *The Voyages of Joshua Slocum*, ed. Walter Teller. Dobbs Ferry, New York: Sheridan House, 1995.

Slocum, Victor. *Capt. Joshua Slocum: The Life and Voyages of America's Best Known Sailor*. Dobbs Ferry, New York: Sheridan House, 1972.

Spencer, Ann. *Alone at Sea: The Adventures of Joshua Slocum*. Toronto: Doubleday Canada, 1998.

Teller, Walter. *Joshua Slocum*. New Brunswick, New Jersey: Rutgers University Press, 1971.

Wolff, Geoffrey. *The Hard Way Around: The Passages of Joshua Slocum*. New York: Alfred A. Knopf, 2010.

IMAGE SOURCES

All images courtesy of the New Bedford Whaling Museum,
Massachusetts, except for the following:

Courtesy of Australian Post

(112)

Nova Scotia Archives

(6) Westport, view of Westport, Digby County, Nova Scotia: 1983-310 number 68760

(12) Launch of the *Forest* from the Churchill Shipyard, Hantsport, NS: 1979-147 66 / negative no.: N-267 N-401

History Collection, Nova Scotia Museum

(2) Westport, NS, showing Peter's Island Light, Digby County, 74.11.3; 20376

Public Domain

(35)

Quentin Casey

(8, 11, 16, 20, 95, 108, 110, 114)

From *Sailing Alone Around the World*, Captain Joshua Slocum, Illustrations by Thomas Fogarty and George Varian

(26, 28, 59, 64, 70, 72, 77, 83)

Courtesy of Sheridan House, from Geoffrey Wolff's *The Hard Way Around*

(17, 18, 19, 22)

INDEX

STORIES OF
OUR PAST SERIES

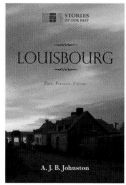

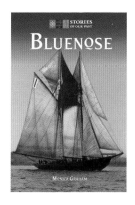

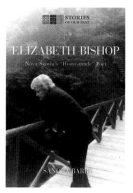